THE RIGHT WAY
TO TEACH
CHESS TO KIDS

Despite being a strong player who is professionally involved in chess, at one time I was clueless when it came to teaching chess to a young beginner, in this case my own son! It was only after getting insights from Richard James, an expert in the field, that the fog started to clear.

Nigel Davies (International Grandmaster)

Also by Richard James
Chess for Kids

THE RIGHT WAY
TO TEACH
CHESS TO KIDS

Richard James

RIGHT WAY

Constable & Robinson Ltd
55–56 Russell Square
London
WC1B 4HP
www.constablerobinson.com

First published by Right Way, an imprint of Constable & Robinson, 2013

A copy of the British Library Cataloguing in Publication Data
is available from the British Library

ISBN: 978-0-7160-2335-7

Printed and bound in the EU

1 3 5 7 9 10 8 6 4 2

CONTENTS

Part Two: A Chess Course for Junior School Age Children

Part Three: Your Next Move

INTRODUCTION

In 1960, when I was ten years old, I found a small plastic chess set on the Christmas tree. My father showed me how the pieces moved, and, the following September, when I started at my secondary school, I began playing against other children. After a few years, when I was able to beat the other boys in my form, my parents introduced me to competitive chess and took me along to the local club. This was how things happened in the 1950s, 60s and 70s.

I started teaching chess privately in 1972 as a result of the interest in chess generated by the Fischer-Spassky match, and in 1975 started Richmond Junior Chess Club with my friend and colleague Mike Fox. The club proved to be very popular and successful, introducing many children to serious competitive chess. In 1993 I had the chance to move into helping local schools run chess clubs. At first it was great to have the opportunity but after a few years I realised that most children were not making much progress and were losing interest after a year or two. Eventually, it hit me that, had chess been popular in primary schools when I was a boy, and had I gone to a club like those where I was teaching, I would have made no progress myself and would not have played chess as an adult.

Now, as far as I'm concerned, chess is the greatest game in the world, and learning the game when and how I did had a dramatic effect on my life. I wanted to make sure that as many children as possible who learnt the moves had a positive experience. So I started asking myself some questions. What if we were starting children too young? What if we were teaching chess in the wrong way? What if we were putting children into tournaments too soon? What if we were promoting chess in the wrong way? So I gave up most of my chess teaching and started reading about child development, about teaching, about parenting (I'm neither a parent nor a qualified teacher), about the philosophy of childhood. I looked at successful methods of teaching other subjects: Kumon maths (worksheets of increasing difficulty), the Suzuki method of teaching music (step by step instruction with regular practice supervised by parents). I looked at how young children in other countries learnt chess and discovered that the methods and philosophy were very different from the informal, unstructured 'let's do chess' approach in use in many schools in the UK.

On returning to chess teaching I decided to be a lot more proactive in talking to parents and discovered that there are very many who want their children to benefit from chess but who have neither the chess knowledge nor the confidence to be able to help them. There are also other parents who, although knowledgeable about chess, confuse their children by introducing more advanced concepts before the basics have been mastered. If you're reading this now you probably fall into one of these categories yourself. If so, this book is written for you.

The book is in three parts. Part One explores the background of chess, how learning it can help children develop skills useful in adult life, and the questions parents and teachers need to take into consideration before setting out to teach children chess; Part Two contains the actual course for teaching chess; while Part Three covers the future possibilities for those children who want to progress further.

PART ONE
YOUR FIRST MOVE

1
WHAT IS CHESS?

Many parents who enquire about chess tuition for their children know little or nothing about chess themselves, but may well have read or heard that 'chess is good for you'.

If you fall into this category this chapter is for you.

A Brief History of Chess

I sometimes ask children how old they think chess is. 'Ten years?', they speculate. 'Twenty years?' 'A hundred years?'

The answer, according to the most popular theory as to the origins of chess' is more like fifteen hundred years.

The earliest forms of the game we now know as chess were first recorded during the sixth century in the Gupta Empire in India. The game was known as 'chaturanga', translating as 'four divisions', the four divisions of the Indian Army: infantry (pawns), cavalry (knights), elephants (bishops) and chariots (rooks), along with the King or Rajah and the Minister or General (queen). It was very specifically a game of military strategy.

By the beginning of the seventh century the game reached Persia, where, under the name 'shatranj' it became very popular. Games and literature from the tenth century onwards still survive.

The moves of the pieces in shatranj were different from the way we play today. The moves of the king, rook and knight were the same, but the queen could only move one square diagonally and the bishop could only jump two squares diagonally, while the pawn could only advance one square on its first move.

The game followed the trade routes to the west and north, reaching southern Europe by the end of the tenth century. By about 1300 changes were made to speed the game up, notably allowing the pawn to move two squares on its first move. At some point towards the end of the fifteenth century the moves of the queen and bishop were changed to make them much more powerful, and the game began to resemble what we know now.

At the same time, the first chess literature was produced, including analysis of openings and endings. Chess was played by the upper classes throughout Europe. The nineteenth century saw the beginning of modern international chess, with matches between the leading English and French players in the 1830s and 1840s and the first international tournament in 1851. The first official world championship match took place in 1886 and, with the introduction of affordable public, followed by private transport, chess competitions at all levels, from international tournaments to inter-club matches and chess leagues, became popular. At the same time chess literature proliferated: books, magazines, and columns in newspapers and a wide variety of periodicals.

The late twentieth century saw further massive changes in the game: the best computer programs were able to beat the strongest human players, internet sites where players could take on opponents from anywhere in the world either in real time or by email became increasingly popular, and chess news and information was readily and freely available at the press of a button.

For most of its history chess has been very much a game for adults, not for children. Chess prodigies such as Paul Morphy in the mid nineteenth century, and Jose Raul Capablanca and Sammy Reshevsky in the early twentieth century hit the headlines, and children from the age of about 11 upwards certainly enjoyed playing, but by and large competitive chess was seen as not being suitable for young children.

The British Under 18 Championship took place for the first time in 1923, and for about thirty years during the 1950s, 1960s and 1970s chess was very popular in secondary schools but then the focus changed from secondary to primary years. In recent years much has been made of claims that 'chess is good for you' and that playing chess can increase your children's IQ and improve their academic results, and this has been one factor in parents and teachers wanting young children to learn the game. The median age for competitors in junior chess tournaments declined by about a year every 5 years between 1950 and 2000.

Perhaps the current fad for early years chess is a historical anomaly and the trend will be reversed. Is chess really suitable for young children? In what ways do children really benefit from chess? If we want to encourage young children to learn chess, how should the game be taught and promoted? These are the questions this book seeks to answer.

A Mathematical Game

Chess is, mathematically speaking, a two-person, zero-sum game with full information. If I win, you lose. If you win, I lose. If you draw, I draw. We both know exactly what pieces both players have and where they are. So it's a game of pure skill, a game so difficult that even the best players in the world make mistakes. The corollary of this is that, sadly, there is, in mathematical terms, no such thing as a good move. Let's assume (safely) that the starting position is a draw with best play. Let's also assume we have a computer which can play perfect chess and will tell us the correct result of any position. (We're many years away from this because of the sheer number of possible positions involved, but there are already databases which will tell us the correct result of any position with six or fewer pieces on the board.) In any position there will then be some (or no) moves which lead to a win, some (or no) moves which lead to a draw, and some (or no) moves which lead to a loss. If you beat me it's because at some point I played a move which changed the assessment from a draw to a win for you. Thus, there are only satisfactory moves, which maintain the status quo, and bad moves, which change it for the worse. Your move could be brilliant, unexpected, profound, beautiful, difficult to find or whatever, but it's only there because I made a mistake which gave you the opportunity. So, the secret of chess is not so much how to play good moves, although that will help, but how to avoid playing bad moves.

2

WHY TEACH CHESS?

Why should you want to teach your children chess? There are many reasons: extrinsic and intrinsic.

It's often said that chess makes kids smarter. You've probably seen this yourself and quite likely it's why you're reading this book. There have been many studies which claim that chess does indeed make kids smarter. However, there are also many other extracurricular activities for your children, which will, it's claimed, have the same effect.

I am unaware of any studies which compare chess with other games, or with other activities such as music, in terms of which is most effective in making kids smarter. Nor am I aware of any studies that set out to discover whether the effect is short term or long term, whether or not the non chess players eventually catch up with, or even overtake, the chess players.

Undoubtedly, if chess is taught correctly, in an age-appropriate way, your children will benefit from it. Because of its complexity we can break chess down into its component parts and ask questions designed to develop specific thinking skills in your children. A later chapter will explain how this might work. But teaching Johnny and Jenny the moves in half an hour so that they can play once a week at their school chess club will have little or no effect.

Also bear in mind that most young children who excel at chess have an above average IQ and very often excel at maths. If you want me to improve your children's IQ I'll teach them how to solve

IQ tests, not how to play chess. If your children are struggling with maths, again I'll teach them maths rather than chess.

You might also ask yourself why you want your children to be smarter, anyway. In a recent book, *How Children Succeed*, American journalist Paul Tough suggests that success in life is more to do with noncognitive skills than how high your IQ is: skills like perseverance, curiosity, conscientiousness, optimism, and self-control. Elizabeth Spiegel (also known as Elizabeth Vicary), chess teacher at IS 318 in Brooklyn, believes that these character traits are more important for chess success than having a high IQ, and that chess is an excellent way of teaching and developing these traits. You need self-control in order to control your impulse to make the first move that comes to mind, and to check that your move is safe before playing it. You need optimism not to give up when you have a bad position, and not to agree a draw in an equal position. You also need optimism and self-confidence to believe that you can do well in your next competition. You need conscientiousness to play your best at all times, especially when playing for a team, and to spend time every day doing the deep practice you need for success. You need curiosity to use your spare time to find out more about chess and how to become a better player. Most of all, you need perseverance and courage in order to deal with failures and setbacks. Everyone makes the occasional mistake, plays the occasional bad game, has the occasional bad tournament, but you need the courage to deal with failure and use blunders and defeats both as a learning opportunity which will make you a stronger player and as a character building opportunity which will make you a stronger person.

In my book *Chess for Kids*, Sam and Alice have to learn these skills along with specific chess skills in order to improve their chess. Sam has to learn to control his impulses and think before he moves. He also has to learn perseverance: to keep going when he makes mistakes or finds something hard to understand. Alice, on the other hand, has to learn to be more positive and more aggressive when she plays chess if she wants to win her games.

There's something else as well. While many people are happy doing a bit of this and a bit of that, there are others who need an all-consuming passion in order to make the most of their lives. For many people, chess, because of its richness, depth and beauty, is that passion.

At one level you can enjoy playing chess with your family and friends, and, for most children who learn the moves, this will be enough. What you also get from chess, if you want it, is much more than that. You can take the game further by joining clubs and playing in competitions, both individual and team. There is a large and very active worldwide network of chess competitions ranging from low level junior events right up to the world championship. Taking part in these events will provide your children with a local, and, if they want, national and international network of like-minded friends. Friendships formed in this way, out of a shared passion rather than just happening to be in the same place at the same time, can, and often do, last a lifetime. Such a network of friendships can also, if you want, be built up in cyberspace: there are many sites where you can play against opponents from all over the world, either in real time or in turn-based games where you are notified by email when it's your move. Beyond that you can get involved in organising tournaments, arbiting at tournaments, club administration or teaching. There's also a whole world of literature, history and heritage to explore. While this isn't for everyone, it can offer something far more valuable than a few extra IQ points. To give your children the chance to experience this, though, you have to give them the best possible start.

So making kids smarter is only one reason for teaching chess. It's also something that can help kids develop beneficial personality traits. More than that, it can give them a lifetime of intellectual stimulation, interest, excitement, and, dare I say it, happiness as well. If you'd like your children to have this opportunity, read on.

3

WHEN TO TEACH CHESS

When should you start your children playing chess? That is one of the biggest questions in this book and there is no one answer.

It depends on what you want to get out of the game: whether your main priority is just to teach them a game they can play for a couple of years at school, to use chess to make your kids smarter, to develop beneficial character traits, or to give them a long-term interest. It depends on your children's intellectual development and maturity. It depends very much on how much help you are able to give them. It also depends on your whole philosophy of childhood: whether you want to fast track your children or let them develop naturally.

Chess and Cognitive Development

Before you make your decision it helps to understand what you can and cannot expect your children to do. The Swiss developmental psychologist Jean Piaget (1896–1980) was among the first researchers in this field. Although his theories have been challenged and in many cases disproved they still have relevance today in considering how we should teach young children chess.

Piaget postulated that children go through four phases of development. The sensorimotor stage, from birth to age 2, need not concern us here. In the preoperational stage (ages 2 to 7), according to Piaget, children are not able to use logical thinking. Next comes the concrete operational stage (ages 7 to 11) during which children are concrete in their thinking and can only think logically with practical aids. Finally, there is the formal operational stage (ages 11 upwards) in which children develop abstract thought and learn to think logically in their minds.

Although I have come across many exceptions, from my general observations of children playing chess this is how it works:

In the preoperational stage (in infant schools or up to Year 2) children will be able to name the pieces, set them up correctly and learn some of the moves but they will struggle with the underlying logic of the game and in dealing with abstract concepts such as checkmate.

In the concrete operational stage (in junior schools from Year 3 to Year 6) children will be able to play a complete game according to the rules and follow rudimentary logic in selecting their moves. ('I moved my queen because you attacked it.' 'I moved there to attack your rook.') but they won't be able to answer questions like 'Why did you play that move rather than this move' coherently. They may appear to play well in simple positions but in situations where there are several things happening at once they'll get confused and play badly.

However, in certain circumstances, children can exceed Piaget's expectations, on occasion by a very long way. Let's take a look at one of the best known and documented stories of chess prodigies.

Polgar and Ericsson

Geniuses are made, not born, according to Laszlo Polgar (1946–), a Hungarian psychologist, who was convinced that children could achieve far more in certain fields than most people believed. He and his wife, Klara, decided to carry out an educational experiment on their children to prove his theory and chose the game of chess as its basis. They homeschooled their three daughters, Zsuzsa (Susan), Zsofia and Judit, all of whom became exceptionally strong players. Susan is now very active as a chess teacher and promoter of chess in the USA, while Judit has been the world's strongest female chess player for many years. Zsofia, perhaps the most talented of the three, was less motivated to play and gave up competitive chess shortly after she married.

I should perhaps add here that I have come across a very small number of children who seem to understand chess at a very young age without being taught. In the same way, there are some children (I was one, as it happens) who learn to read very young without being taught. Perhaps your children will pick up chess like that, but don't assume that they will.

In recent years the theory of Swedish Professor of Psychology Anders Ericsson that most people could achieve expertise in their chosen field with 10,000 hours of deep practice over 10 years has gained wide currency. Within chess this is considered to be reaching Grandmaster level. While I don't believe for a moment that everyone has that potential, it is clear that deep practice (practice specifically designed to target areas of improvement) is what makes a good chess player, just as it is necessary if you want to become a good tennis player or a good pianist. If you look at the methods used by Laszlo Polgar in teaching chess to his daughters you'll see that deep practice was very much what he was doing.

While I would expect few, if any, readers of this book to take that route, it is clear that serious practice is necessary for your children to achieve success at the game. Exactly what that entails will be discussed in a later chapter.

So when should you start?

As we've seen, social chess is, in Piagetian terms, a concrete operational activity, suitable for children from age 7 upwards. Tournament chess at an adult level is a formal operational activity, suitable for children from age 11 upwards. However, with regular deep practice, or perhaps a touch of genius, children can attain these levels earlier, sometimes much earlier, than Piaget would have you believe.

There are, in principle, a number of reasons why you might want to start your children with chess at an early age:

Younger children are more likely to be drawn to chess: board games appeal more to younger children than to older children, and the chess pieces themselves with their different shapes are particularly attractive to young children.

Young children enjoy and benefit from playing all sorts of games with their friends, and school chess clubs provide them with the opportunity to play chess in this way.

Older children might not want to learn because they associate board games with younger children.

Children who start young may gain more academic benefit from chess than children who start when they are older.

Children who start young are more likely to become very strong players than children who start later.

But there are also some potential disadvantages:

The younger children start the longer it will take them to learn the game: they may get frustrated by the slowness of their progress and perhaps give up because they find some concepts difficult to understand.

The younger children start the more likely it is that chess will just be a childish craze for them and they will soon lose interest.

The younger children start the more likely it is that they will give up as they get older because they associate chess with childhood and see it as a children's game.

The younger children start the more help and support they will need from their parents: children who start young and do not get parental support will, regardless of their talent or potential, do less well than children who are getting constructive and proactive help at home.

Older children will, when they're ready, be able to teach themselves, and will not need parents to stay with them at tournaments.

Older children might be more likely to have the self-awareness to be able to use chess to develop noncognitive skills.

Many adults enjoy chess because of its aesthetic beauty, its scope for serious study and scientific analysis, its literature, its history and its heritage: all aspects of the game that cannot really be appreciated by young children. Children who start young and give up quickly will never get to experience this side of chess.

Some parents take something approaching a 'Tiger Mom' approach. They believe in starting children young and want their children to excel at everything they do. They expect commitment, maturity and a seriousness of purpose from their children. If this is your approach to parenting then starting your children young would be an excellent idea, and chess would make an excellent fit for your parenting style. A recent book (*Chess Is Child's Play: Teaching Techniques That Work* by Laura Sherman and Bill Kilpatrick) even suggests that children as young as two could start some chess-related activities.

On the other hand, there are many who prefer 'slow' parenting to 'fast' parenting, who believe that children are increasingly doing too much too soon, that children would be better off not starting formal schooling until they are 6 or even 7, that children benefit more from outdoor play than from indoor play, and more from unstructured play than from structured play. If you are attracted by this philosophy (associated with Jean-Jacques Rousseau, who was himself an avid, but not very good, chess player), you'd be better off encouraging your children to play later rather than earlier: at 8, 9 or even 10. At that age they'll still need some support and encouragement from you, but not as much as if they started younger.

Many parents are, for a wide variety of perfectly valid reasons, unable to provide a lot of help and support for their children's chess. If this is true for you it would be better not to do too much until your children are old enough to teach themselves, which would probably be at about 12 or 13. My parents bought me a chess set when I was 10, but were unable to help beyond teaching me the moves. When they saw I was really interested in the game they bought me a book so that I could teach myself.

If your children's school has a chess club, or there is a junior chess club in your area, you might well want to teach them the moves so that they can join. If your school offers courses for beginners, again you might want to sign your children up. If there is no junior chess in your area (and sadly this is true in many parts of the UK) you might want to wait until they're old enough to join an adult chess club or play on the internet (but note that there is an enormous gap between social chess and adult club chess, and that adult chess clubs are, for various reasons, not always suitable for children).

So there are all sorts of reasons why you might want your children to learn chess at any age, but do remember that the younger they start the more help they will need from you. How well young children do in chess competitions is much more a result of the quality and quantity of parental support than their own talent.

If you don't feel qualified to teach your children, read on. I'm here to help.

4
HOW TO TEACH CHESS

Rousseau put forward the theory that, up to the age of about 12, children are guided by emotions and impulses. They only start to develop reason between the ages of 12 and 16. One hundred and fifty or so years later, Piaget put forward his theory that (in very simplistic terms) children could develop simple, concrete logic from about 7 or 8, but would only develop more complex reasoning skills from about 11 or 12.

It's natural that, when children first learn chess, they will be guided by emotions and impulses when choosing their moves. If you were learning a new game, you'd probably be guided in the same way before trying to work out the principles of good play.

You won't get very far in chess just with emotions and impulses, though. Young children usually learn best by repetition and reinforcement, by memory and mimicry. In a general way, if they play regularly against good players who are using appropriate strategies, they will learn these strategies as well, especially if the strategies are being explained to them. If, on the other hand, they play regularly against novices who are using inappropriate strategies, they will just learn how to play badly. Children can learn certain endgame techniques: for example, how to force checkmate with king and queen against king, by memory. We might (and often do, but perhaps we shouldn't) teach children openings by memory. What children learn in a lesson, whether at school or at home, needs to be reinforced through games or puzzles: otherwise it will be forgotten, or, sometimes worse, inaccurately half-remembered.

But in order to play well – well enough for it to be worth their while continuing playing – children of primary school age need to learn the cognitive and noncognitive skills necessary to process complex technical information. Many children who learn the moves at about 6 or 7 are entranced with the game. This gives parents and teachers who want to take this route (and some will have, entirely reasonably, a different concept of childhood) a fantastic opportunity to use their children's love of chess to help them develop these skills.

By following an appropriate curriculum, children will be able to learn a wide range of thinking skills involving logic, reasoning and decision making. They'll be developing their visuospatial development by learning to look at a chessboard. Most importantly of all, they'll be able to develop noncognitive skills such as impulse control, concentration, determination and courage.

There are many approaches to teaching chess: the one that is right for your children will depend to a great extent on their age and stage of development.

Personally, I see few advantages and many potential disadvantages in teaching children in the pre-operational stage very much about chess. There are many other simpler strategy games which are appropriate for very young children. If your children see you playing and want to find out more you could start by telling them the names of the pieces and maybe how to set them up for the start of the game. Then you could play very simple games with the easier pieces: firstly the rook, then the bishop and finally the queen. At this age chess is best taught one to one, parent to child, rather than within a group. No need to rush: just do chess whenever they want to do it. Some children will pick up chess all in one go by just watching (Capablanca claimed that he learnt chess at the age of 4 by watching his father play, pointed out an illegal move and beat him twice) but most will not.

Much of this book is devoted to recommendations for children in the concrete operational stage of development (usually from 7 upwards but children as young as 5 can, if they are sufficiently mature, learn in this way). Reference is made to my website chessKIDS academy (www.chesskids.org.uk or www.chesskids.me.uk) and a copy of my book *Chess for Kids*, the companion volume to this book, will also be useful.

The course will be outlined in more detail in Part Two. While some children of this age will be able to learn the whole of chess, just like that, most children are incremental learners who will do best by picking up concepts one by one. I therefore recommend a step by step approach for children of this age, learning one piece at a time and one cognitive skill at a time, and only moving on when the children are very familiar with the piece and have also mastered the associated thinking skills. After all, children learn other subjects step by step. In maths, they learn addition before subtraction, multiplication before division. They learn to work with small numbers before moving on to larger numbers. They learn to read one letter or sound at a time. Trying to teach all the rules of chess in one session will leave many children confused just as trying to teach them addition, subtraction, multiplication and division in one session will.

To get full benefit from the game your children should be playing regularly, ideally 10–15 minutes a day, as well as solving puzzles on a regular basis to develop chessboard vision. If they are learning chess at school or at a club you will need to support their learning by reinforcing what they have learnt in their lesson if you want them to benefit from their studies. It's just the same as learning a musical instrument: if you don't practise every day you're not going to make very much progress.

Children who are not getting help at home will lose continually against children whose parents are supporting them. Ideally, children of this age should spend at least a year learning chess step by step, either at home or in a beginners' group at a school or chess club, before joining a competitive chess club.

Children who are learning chess in the formal operational stage (at secondary school rather than primary school age) might still benefit from aspects of the step by step approach but by now they will be acquiring or learning the skills to teach themselves chess with much less parental help as well as the complex abstract logic required to understand what's happening in a game.

It's your choice: teach them the moves but don't push them at all until they're older, or teach them the moves and use the game as a learning tool to accelerate their cognitive and noncognitive development while giving them the chance to join clubs and take part in competitions.

5
WHERE TO TEACH CHESS

In this chapter we're considering 'where' children should learn chess loosely in terms of the environment in which children learn and the different media which could be used. In theory you have a lot of choices, but which will be best for you and your children?

If you have a choice of environments, your decision will depend on whether your children are independent learners, who work better on their own, competitive learners, who like to work in a group competing with their friends, or collaborative learners, who like to work in a group helping each other.

The obvious way for most children to learn is from a relative, usually a parent, but it could be a grandparent, uncle or aunt, cousin or older sibling. If your children are just learning the moves in half an hour or so then it doesn't really matter, but I don't believe this is the right way for most young children to learn the game.

If we're talking about weekly lessons for a period of, say, six to twelve months, along with regular practice and reinforcement, which is what you'll need if your children are to get any real benefit from learning chess, you'll want to think carefully about how to do it.

In many ways you are your children's best teacher. You know better than anyone else how their minds work, how to read them, how to tell whether they've had enough or want more, whether they're finding something too easy or too hard. If you're a chess player yourself (you don't have to be a good player, but you'll need to know enough to recognise good play when you see it) teaching your child should be no problem as long as you follow the principles outlined in this book. I sometimes meet older children who tell me they hate chess because their father taught them when they were younger and beat them every time: so beware of acting the competitive dad in this way. There will be advice on how to play against your children later in this book.

If you're not a good chess player yourself, there's no need to worry. You can still teach your children as long as you're prepared to make the effort to learn yourself, and to keep one step ahead, making sure you fully understand every concept before teaching it. There are many children in school chess clubs who get the basics wrong: they might set the board up incorrectly or refer to rooks as 'castles'. If you don't teach them well they'll stand very little chance of making progress.

If you don't feel confident about teaching your children yourself you might want to consider hiring a private tutor. You might also feel that your children might respond better to someone they don't know so well. Most chess teachers are strong players who prefer working with older and stronger children, and may not have the necessary experience and skills to teach young beginners. They may teach them too quickly and fail to check that concepts have been fully understood. They will also tend to provide technical information rather than teach the cognitive skills children require in order to process technical information efficiently. Chess lessons of this nature, for young beginners, should, if used at all, be an adjunct to what you're doing at home rather than a replacement. Children also need a real enthusiasm for chess in order to benefit from private tuition. I've wasted a lot of time (and parents have wasted a lot of money) in the past doing private tuition for young children who do no chess at all at home between one lesson and the next and who have no real interest in the game. Chess teachers cannot make young children good at chess: only you, the parents, can do that.

One possible problem with one-to-one tuition of beginners is that it can become rather intense, especially for children whose learning style is competitive or collaborative rather than independent. Perhaps you could teach a younger sibling at the same time, or teach one of your children's friends? There are many advantages in this arrangement. Children can work together helping each other solve problems, or compete against each other to see who is better at solving problems. They will also have a peer to play against rather than having to play their teacher every time. The two players can play together against the teacher, consulting and discussing the moves. This will enable them to avoid the most obvious mistakes as well as teaching them how to consider alternatives before choosing their move. There are also many social benefits in being able to learn something together with a friend.

Some schools teach chess to complete beginners, either on the curriculum or as an extra-curricular activity, which is fine. After-school or lunchtime chess clubs are not necessarily the place to go if you don't know the moves: by and large they will be aimed at children who have already learnt the moves at home. Complete beginners really need to be taught one to one or in a group with other complete beginners, and school chess clubs with maybe thirty or forty children, most of whom can play a complete game, are not really suitable for children who don't know the moves.

You might also have a junior chess club in your area: these tend to run at a rather more serious level than school clubs and can be seen as a bridge between the school club and adult competitive chess. Some junior clubs will claim they take beginners: but they may mean children who know the moves but nothing else rather than complete beginners. You'd also need to ask whether or not they have separate facilities for novices rather than just putting them in a room full of serious players where the lessons will be too hard for them to understand and they'll be expected to do things like record their games and use clocks. Ideally, junior clubs would have a separate section, in a different room or at a different time, for less experienced players who are not able to play chess at school: but do make enquiries first and perhaps go along to see for yourself. Children can easily be put off chess for life by being put into an unsuitable environment where they won't understand the instruction and will lose all their games.

You're probably aware of the principle of VAK (Visual Auditory Kinaesthetic), and the idea that some students learn best from visual cues (what they see), some from auditory cues (what they hear), and some from kinaesthetic cues (actually doing something). A good chess teacher will be using all three methods: showing you the moves, describing and explaining them and getting you to make them yourself.

You also have a wide choice of different media to use in teaching your children chess. Your children's unique learning style will determine which combination you use. Traditionally, there are chess books. There's a wide range of books for children on the market. There are many books for beginners, all of which take different approaches. I recommend those which use a step by step approach and would add that books written by specialist chess teachers (particularly those who work with younger children) are usually a better choice than those written by very strong players. In particular, beware of books which claim to be for kids but are in effect books for lower level adults with added cartoons. These books are often excellent for serious competitive players but, despite their titles, unsuitable for beginners.

These days, many children prefer screen-based instruction to books, and again you have a choice. There are a number of DVDs available for beginners, but again be careful that they really are aimed at young children rather than adult novices. There are also various software titles available specifically aimed at young children. A number of websites offer a range of instructional materials for early years learners. My website chessKIDS academy (www.chesskids.org.uk or www.chesskids.me.uk) includes a complete course in the form of interactive lessons, each of which is reinforced by a quiz, which will take the student from learning the moves through to adult club standard. There are also videos accompanying the earlier lessons, many other games and puzzles, and several computer programs, one of which is set up to play some of the mini-games described in the course you'll find later in the book. You'll also find a lot of educational chess videos on YouTube and elsewhere, but, inevitably, the standard is variable. If your children are starting young, though, you'll probably want to restrict their screen time. And because of the game's complexity, young children cannot teach themselves chess in any meaningful way. Whatever media you use, you will need to supervise your children's learning.

6

WHO SHOULD LEARN CHESS?

Who are the children who would benefit most from chess? In secondary schools you might be surprised: it's sometimes the children you least expect, but in primary schools there's a distinct pattern.

All children can enjoy and benefit from playing strategy games, although some will, at this age, find chess too hard. I've taught children who haven't taken to chess but have enjoyed playing simpler strategy games such as the African game Mancala (Oware). The methods recommended in this book include various mini-games which children will enjoy: they only need to move on if and when they are ready to do so.

Most primary school age chess players who are successful in competitions outside school have several things in common:

1. They are academically successful: typically excelling at mathematics and other activities involving logic and reasoning. Some children who do well at chess are strong academic all-rounders who excel at all subjects, while others are the maths specialists who may not do so well at English or other subjects requiring creativity and imagination. Many parents of young chess players tell me their children enjoy reading non-fiction books but it's hard to get them to read fiction. They will have an above average IQ but not necessarily genius level. However, children who are not academically strong can still enjoy playing chess and will often get a lot out of it.

2. They are competitive in nature: they want to succeed, want to win their games, want to be the best that they can be. The children who cry when they lose are often those who eventually become strong players. If you don't like losing you have an incentive to learn to play better. The children who like moving the pieces round the board without having much interest in who wins will be unlikely to retain an interest for very long. Having said that, children who lack the killer instinct will often prefer the non-competitive side of chess, and enjoy solving puzzles at home while not feeling the need or having the confidence to play competitively.

3. They have supportive and proactive parents who will take them to chess clubs and tournaments, arrange tuition and ensure they spend time practising at home: who have the time and the inclination to do everything they can to help their children.

4. They have regular access to a strong chess player who can help them, play with them and go through their games. This could be a family member, a friend of the family, a teacher at school (although not many primary schools have strong players on the staff) or a professional chess teacher.

5. They have a seriousness of purpose: the maturity to switch off from being a child and become an adult when they're sitting at a chessboard: to control their impulses and emotions, to look at everything on the board and to use logic and reasoning to choose their moves. To be a successful higher level tournament player requires complex thinking skills along with emotional maturity. This, for so many children, is where they come unstuck and fail to make progress.

Chess is at the moment very much male-dominated. Many school chess clubs are close to 100 per cent boys. As Laszlo Polgar demonstrated, though, girls can and do excel at the game. We'll look at some possible reasons for the male domination of chess and ways in which we can get more girls interested in the next chapter.

Chess, by its nature, often appeals to more introverted people who prefer a more solitary pursuit taking place in a quiet environment with a limited amount of social interaction with others. Many extraverts also play chess, but they tend to be the 'joiners' who have a lot of other interests. For this reason, school chess clubs are not always as quiet as some would like, and this may possibly deter some children who would otherwise get a lot out of chess. Chess can also provide a competitive outlet for those children who struggle with physical sports. Many children who do well at physical sports also play chess and in many schools the same children often play in both the chess and the football teams, but again the sporty children will be spending a lot of time on their other activities and may have less time for chess. In Chapter 8 we'll look in more detail at chess and special needs, and, in particular, chess and the autistic spectrum.

7

CHESS: BOYS AND GIRLS

I'm often asked why so few girls and women play chess. In my view there are two underlying reasons which go some way to explaining why chess seems to appeal more to boys than to girls.

Families often see chess as a male activity, so fathers teach their sons how to play, partly as a form of male bonding, but don't always teach their daughters. Some families, on the other hand, are games players who regularly sit round the table playing board games including chess. In other families there's a strong chess background with parents and children all being serious players. These families will teach their daughters to play along with their sons, with no discrimination.

If you go into a school, though, most of the boys will tell you they know how to play, but most of the girls will tell you they don't know how to play. This is one reason why most school chess clubs are nearly all boys, and if girls are in a small minority they're quite likely not to stay very long.

There's another reason as well, though. If you spend time in a primary school watching how children interact with each other in lessons, and, even more so, at play, you'll find a big difference. (There has been much debate about to what extent this is due to nurture rather than nature, but further discussion is beyond the scope of this book.) Most girls like to chat with their friends, or play non-competitive, cooperative games. Most boys prefer football, chasing games, fighting games and role-playing war games. In the past, boys played Cowboys and Indians, or Cops and Robbers: these days boys play the same game but are more likely to call it Call of Duty instead. Some schools are squeamish about male aggression and ban fighting or war games. If you talk to the girls they'll tell you they hate the boys, and if you talk to the boys they'll tell you they hate the girls. They actually mean 'don't understand' rather than 'hate' but lack the sophistication to know the difference.

There's another difference between the typical boy and the typical girl as well. Boys tend on the whole to be impulsive: to play the first move they think of, whereas girls are often indecisive and spend a long time deciding what to play, not because they're thinking about the position in depth but just because they can't make up their mind. The characters of Sam and Alice in *Chess for Kids* are stereotypical in many ways. As your children read the book you can discuss these issues with them. Do they see themselves as more like Sam? If so, how can they learn to control their impulses? Or perhaps they see themselves as more like Alice. If so, how can they learn to be more decisive?

Many girls (and some boys), when they first play chess, are more interested in making pretty patterns with their pawns than with trying to find good moves. I've also seen girls burying their queen in the corner behind the pawns, saying 'The queen's the mummy so she has to stay at home to look after her babies' while marching their king up the board, saying 'The king's the daddy so he has to go out to work'. Apart from its lack of political correctness, this is not a very successful chess strategy.

Chess, as we have seen, started life as a war game. It's also, by its nature, competitive: someone wins and someone else loses. Girls are, by and large, less happy with this than boys, and less competitive than boys. Should we encourage girls to be more competitive? Or should we teach chess to girls in a non-competitive way, with emphasis on working together and solving puzzles? You might even think it's not entirely a bad thing that an activity which correlates strongly with academic success should be more popular with boys than with girls. If you're a parent or teacher of girls it's your choice.

Chess organisers do a lot to encourage more girls to take part in competitive chess. Most tournaments have prizes for the top girl and there are also separate tournament for girls. While there are some who consider this to be reverse discrimination and find it patronising, it is undoubtedly successful, at least in the short term, in encouraging more girls to compete. Boys tend to take part because they want to win while girls are more interested in the idea of sharing an interest with their friends, so it's often a good idea to encourage a group of girls to get together to join a club or take part in competitions.

8

CHESS AND SPECIAL NEEDS

Between 20–25 per cent of children are classified as 'special needs' and diagnosed with a wide range of neurological conditions. For many of these children, chess can have a dramatic effect on their lives. But it is exactly these children, who may well have the most to gain from chess, who will, in many cases, and for a variety of reasons, not consider joining a school chess club, or perhaps not enjoy it if they do join.

These conditions cover four main areas: learning difficulties (for instance, dyslexia), physical problems (for instance, dyspraxia), problems with attention, concentration and behaviour (for instance, ADHD) and difficulties with communication, socialisation and relationships (for instance, Asperger Syndrome). Frequently, children with problems in one area will have problems in another area as well. Some (but not all) children in each of these areas will gain enormous benefit from chess.

Although children with more general learning difficulties will probably struggle with chess, many children with dyslexia, and also other conditions such as Non-Verbal Learning Disorder can and do excel at chess. Indeed, many dyslexics have a very strong visuospatial awareness which can come in very useful over the chessboard. Although some of these children may not enjoy reading, there are now many other ways of accessing chess information, so this is not necessarily going to be a handicap. For those who may not meet with a lot of academic success, success at chess, using their visuospatial talents, will give their self-esteem an enormous boost.

Children with problems such as dyspraxia which impair physical abilities may not be able to excel at many sports, but chess will provide them with a competitive arena in which they may be able to excel. They might be the last to get picked for the football team, but if, while their friends are kicking balls around, they are studying chess, they'll be the first to be picked for the chess team. Not being good at sports is tough, especially for boys where popularity is often defined by success on the sports field, and, for these children, chess will be one of the few outlets available for their competitive spirit.

I'd be the first to admit that having an ADHD child in your classroom or chess club can be a nightmare, but many children with a diagnosis of ADHD, while easily distracted and unable to concentrate on something that doesn't interest them, can hyperfocus on something in which they are really interested. And that something might just be chess. So give chess a try – it might just be the spark that will help them concentrate and focus, and perhaps understanding that they can pay attention during a chess game will help them pay attention in the classroom as well.

For many children with communication and socialisation problems, chess can be something very special. Children with a diagnosis on the autistic spectrum often prefer quiet, low-stimulation environments. Some of them also have a high IQ, a strong logical-mathematical brain and powers of intense focus. For children like this, chess is the ideal hobby. Several prominent chess players have diagnoses of Asperger Syndrome, while many others have significant autistic traits, and, in my experience, the chess world is, by and large, very tolerant of differences. The child who finds himself alone and out of place in the real world may well find, in the world of chess, somewhere he will feel at home, among like-minded people. Chess isn't for all autistic spectrum children, but, for some, discovering chess can be a life-changing experience.

Yet many of these children may not consider joining a chess club. The dyslexic children may be accustomed to academic failure and think chess is not for them. The dyspraxic children may be switched off to the whole idea of competition by their lack of sporting success. The ADHD children may feel they won't be able to concentrate and will get into trouble. The AS children will often be non-joiners who don't volunteer for group activities, and if they do join their school chess club they may find that it isn't always as quiet or predictable as they might like.

9
CHESS IN PRIMARY SCHOOLS

I spent fifteen years involved with after-school and lunchtime chess clubs, mostly in primary and prep schools, in the London Borough of Richmond upon Thames, one of the more affluent London boroughs. It became clear to me after a few years that these clubs were only giving children a short-term interest in the game and that most children made little progress. So I decided to move on, while looking at how schools could promote chess in a different way. This book is, in part, a result of my decision.

What happens, at least in Richmond, is that many schools choose to run an after-school chess club, and, in many cases, appoint a professional chess teacher to help them run it. In some schools, there's a member of the school staff in the room as well, in other schools not. The children in the club fall into several categories. There are children who join the club because their parents would like them to learn the moves but are unable to teach them at home. There are children whose parents have taught them the moves so that they can join the school club, but who never play or get any help at home. There are children whose parents are keen to help them improve, but don't know where to start. There are children whose parents are fairly knowledgeable about chess and are able to help them and provide them with some useful advice. There may also be a few more serious players who go to junior chess clubs and play in tournaments. There are children aged between 7 and 11, some with no experience at all and some with four years' experience or more. There are children who want to play seriously and learn more about chess, children who just want to play informal games with their friends, and perhaps children who don't want to play chess at all.

Consider the analogy of a swimming pool. You might go to the swimming pool because you want to learn to swim. You might go because you want to have fun splashing around in the shallow end with your friends. You might go because you want to exercise by swimming up and down in a fairly serious way. Or you might want to train for serious competition. All these, of course, are absolutely fine, but you can't have all of them (or even more than one) happening at the same time.

There are several chess services schools could offer. Which you should choose, and how you should go about it, will depend on a number of factors: your catchment area and intake, the size of your school, the ethos of your school (competitive or non-competitive), whether or not you have a chess player on the staff, and so on.

You might decide you'd like to teach chess to beginners. You then have a choice: do you want every child in the school to learn or make it an optional extra? Do you want to teach chess to improve children's cognitive skills, or to enable them to compete against other schools? If you want every child to learn chess you'll need to put it on the curriculum. You'll need a structured course to do this: there's one in this book and suggestions as to other possible courses in the Resources chapter at the end of the book. You might not want to set compulsory homework but you'd be well advised to have course materials available for parents so that they can support their children at home should they choose to do so. You might want to employ a professional chess teacher, but you may well be better off using a member of staff with an interest in chess. At this level an understanding of how to control a class, how to teach and how children learn is more important than chess strength. Professional chess teachers will often go too quickly, failing to ensure that the whole class has understood the topic before moving on. It's only necessary for the teacher to be one step ahead of the class to teach young beginners. I should add at this point that Chess in Schools and Communities (www.chessinschools.co.uk) is doing a great job putting chess into schools in the UK, at the time of writing working mostly in deprived areas, and empowering teachers to run chess clubs and classes themselves. Please visit their website for further information.

You might think that more children will benefit if you use a wider range of strategy games rather than just chess. Some children will find chess too hard and may benefit more from simpler games (although my course introduces chess through a series of simpler mini-games). Other children might prefer games which offer less competition and more opportunity for collaboration, although there are ways to teach chess collaboratively and non-competitively. You might think there are advantages in providing children with a wider range of cultural references by offering a curriculum introducing children to different board and strategy games from around the world. You might also want to look at cross-curricular links, which we'll consider in more detail in the next chapter. The choice, as always, is yours.

If you want to teach chess to beginners as an extra-curricular activity, through a lunchtime or after-school club, you'll have similar choices to make. You might also want to decide whether you're targeting complete beginners or children who know the moves but nothing else: and which course you use or where you start in the course will depend on this choice. You might also want to decide whether you want to be proactive in selecting children to learn chess, for instance by inviting the more introverted non-joiners to take part. You might want to encourage some of your children on the autistic spectrum to join, or dyspraxic children who struggle with physical activities. You might want to provide specific encouragement for girls to take part. You might also want to decide whether you're promoting chess as a competitive activity or as a non-competitive way of developing cognitive skills.

Some schools have started chess clubs by selecting those children who excel at maths, or have been encouraged to start clubs to demonstrate to OFSTED that they are providing activities to stretch their most able pupils. There is also a lot of scope for using chess as a form of curriculum enhancement for gifted and talented students.

You might decide – and this will probably be the most popular choice – that you want to provide children who know how to play chess with the opportunity to play casual games with their friends. A long time ago, when I was a boy, children would bring their own chess sets into school, but, sadly, this no longer seems to be the case. Most children in most school chess clubs, in my experience, are only really interested in playing on an informal basis, although there are various things we can do to encourage them to take the game more seriously. Let me say at the start that, in my opinion, there's not a lot of point in doing chess if children only have the opportunity to play once a week. If you want to run a group for casual players that's absolutely fine. If you like, this is the chess equivalent of splashing around in the shallow end. You won't need a professional chess teacher for this, in the same way that you'll need a lifeguard rather than a professional swimming coach for the kids in the shallow end. All you need is a teacher or parent who knows enough to answer simple questions like 'is this checkmate?' You might want to ensure in some way that children actually know how the pieces move before joining a group of this nature. You'd also want to get the message across to both parents and children that you are only running an entry-level informal group, and that children who want to take the game further should perhaps join their local junior chess club (assuming there is one), who should be able to provide you with flyers or advertise in your school newsletter or on your website. It would also be good if children had access to chess sets at all times, not just once a week for the chess club. Even if they were available during Wet Play it would help. I appreciate that, when young children are involved, if they are not supervised, pieces might get damaged or lost, so you might need to ensure adequate supervision.

You might also like to choose a halfway house between this and the next option by giving your children some low-level experience of competitive chess. This could be done by entering the UK Chess Challenge, playing matches against other schools, or even inter-form or inter-house matches.

The third product you could offer is intermediate level tuition: this would be appropriate if you want to see yourself as a 'chess school'. If you get this right you'll be able to participate successfully in competitions against other local schools and your pupils will be able to take part in tournaments successfully. This is, I guess, what schools expect if they employ a professional chess teacher. But, in reality, it doesn't quite happen like this, which is why I stopped most of my teaching in school chess clubs. Here's why.

Firstly, a lot of the children enjoy playing chess with their friends but have no interest in learning to play better. If you go into a chess club and ask the children whether chess is a game of luck or of skill, a lot of them will tell you it's just a game of luck. Snakes and Ladders with more complicated rules. And they're quite happy with it like that. They don't want to be told how to play properly any more than the kids splashing around in the shallow end want a swimming coach to tell them how to swim properly.

Secondly, a lot of children are either doing no chess at all at home, or playing the occasional game with a relation who may well be a weak player who will give them bad habits. There's no way children with this background will make much progress. Children of secondary school age will be able to teach themselves to play well should they wish to do so, but children of primary school age will be too young to do this. They will even argue with you, on occasion, that their dad said something different from what you told them, and because he's their dad he must be right. A child who is learning the piano will need to practise regularly in order to make progress: it's exactly the same with chess.

Thirdly, because there is no repetition or reinforcement, children will find it hard to remember and put into practice what they have learnt at the club. Typically, they will half remember or misunderstand the contents of the lesson, and this will often just leave them confused. Several years ago, I was running a junior tournament. After the first three games a boy who had lost all his games came up to me to tell me his opponents were all cheating. When I asked him what they were doing he replied that their knights were all jumping over his pieces, and that his chess teacher had told him that knights can't jump. I asked the name of his chess teacher, and, as I knew he would, he gave me the name of a very strong and well respected grandmaster.

So there you are. There are three chess products you could offer your pupils: basic tuition for beginners, somewhere for children to play casual games with their friends, and intermediate level tuition for more serious players. (There are a few very ambitious schools, mostly in the private sector, who offer higher level tuition.) It is entirely reasonable to offer all of these, none of them, or any combination, depending on what you want out of chess. What is not going to work so well is to say 'let's do chess' and see who turns up. Trying to be everything to everyone ends up being nothing very much to anyone.

To provide basic tuition you need a good teacher and a structured course: you don't need a strong player any more than you need Stephen Hawking to teach your children that 2+2=4. You also need to provide materials to enable parents to help their children at home. (You may be using a course with workbooks for children which they can take home.)

Ideally, children will be able to play casual games at break or lunchtime but they may need to be supervised. You might like to have chess sets available in common areas for children to use. You could also buy a giant chess set for the playground. If you want to offer an after-school club for casual and low-level competitive chess this could be run by a teacher or parent volunteer with some knowledge of chess. It might also be helpful to employ a professional chess coach who could take a few of the stronger players aside. It would help if you could provide advice for parents on how to help their children along with flyers or website links to local junior chess clubs and coaches.

If you want to offer intermediate level tuition you'll need a serious and knowledgeable player who is able to communicate his or her passion for chess to children. This might, if you're lucky, be a teacher or parent, but is more likely to be a professional chess coach. If you want a professional chess coach, though, you'll have to decide about funding. Suppose you have forty children who want to join an after-school club, but only ten are serious. I'd only be interested in teaching the serious ones, but you'd probably have to charge all forty to afford to pay me.

Chess in primary schools can bring so many benefits, helping to develop children's academic, cognitive and noncognitive skills, improving their psychological well-being, and, in some cases, giving them a lifelong interest, and maybe even a career. I'd really like to see every school in the country active in promoting chess. But doing so without thought as to what you want to achieve may well end up being counterproductive. Like other subjects, chess is best taught to young children one step at a time, with plenty of repetition and reinforcement. Children who learn the moves in half an hour, play a couple of games at home and then once a week at the school chess club will get little or no benefit from the game.

10

CHESS AND CROSS-CURRICULAR LINKS

The exceptional cultural depth of chess makes it ideal for crosscurricular links with almost any subject. A school that is really keen on chess can use many of these links both to enrich its own curriculum and to enhance its students' passion for the game. Parents who are homeschooling a child with a particular interest in chess could devise a whole curriculum based around their favourite game.

There's only room to skim the surface here, but if you're interested I'd point you in the direction of the series of books written by Alexey Root, even though they are geared towards the US school curriculum.

Maths

As you would expect, given the correlation between maths and chess success at this age, there are many mutual connections. There are whole courses in use in Canada and elsewhere combining the two disciplines.

For a start, you can use a chessboard to provide a graphic demonstration of multiplication tables up to 8x8. If you want to take this further, make a larger chequered board. You can then use the board to demonstrate anything to do with squares, rectangles or, at a pinch, right-angled triangles. From the perspective of a chess player, a king on e1 moving to e2 or d2 is just one move, but if you measure it, d2 is further away – cue Pythagoras. Get children to tell you the number of squares round the perimeter of the board. Most primary school children will see four sides with eight squares on each side and tell you the answer's 32. If you ask them to count they'll include the starting square twice and tell you it's 29. Can they work out the error in their thinking? If a knight can get from a1 to h8 in six moves, can it get there in seven? If not, why not? How many squares are there in total on a chessboard (including larger squares as well as smaller squares)? How many squares are there on an n by n board? What's the general formula for working this out? Then we have the values of the pieces. Most children enjoy adding up the points of the pieces both players have captured to see who's ahead. Help them to understand the concept of profit and loss: if they trade a knight for a rook they make a profit of 2 points but if they trade a rook and bishop for a queen they make a loss of one point. Children are also learning the mathematical concept of coordinates when they learn the names of the squares.

There are many chess puzzles which could be considered mathematical in nature. Can you solve the Eight Officers Problem? Can you place eight queens (use pawns if you like) on the board so that there is no more than one on any rank, file or diagonal? How far can you get with the Knight Tour? A knight has to visit every square on the board once only: possible but not easy. If you can do that, try a re-entrant knight tour, where you have to be able to move from the finishing square back to the starting square.

If you place one grain of rice on the first square of the board, two grains on the second square, four grains on the third square and so on, doubling the grains of rice every time, how many grains of rice will you need in total for the whole board? Clue – it's a very large number.

There's much more (along with many other goodies) in Canadian writer Jeff Coakley's wonderful chess puzzle books for kids (see the Resources chapter at the end for further details).

English

Studies have demonstrated that chess can increase children's reading scores as well as their maths scores. Children who are passionate about chess will want to read about it: books, magazines or websites. We'll consider elsewhere how chess can be used to improve children's verbalisation skills by encouraging them to talk about the position on the board and what they plan to do. Chess can be used as a basis for creative writing: get children to write a story with a chess theme (*Chess for Kids* might serve as an example). The opportunities for children to use chess to develop their imagination in this way are limitless. Look, for instance, at *Through the Looking Glass*, at some of the Harry Potter books (and the first movie) and much else. You could also use chess to develop factual writing skills: can they write an explanation of the *en passant* rule, or how to force checkmate with two rooks? Or they could write an essay about their favourite chess player, or about some aspect of chess history that interests them. (I'm very big on teaching children about chess history and culture as well as how to play good moves.)

Arts and Crafts

The iconography of chess is another really powerful aspect of the game. Most children are fascinated by the different pieces and like to look at different chess sets. A quick search on the internet will find much of interest. All children could design their own chess pieces: it's not just making them look nice but making them playable by being easily distinguished from each other. Older children could even try to make their own chess set in craft lessons. Children could also design costumes for a living chess game (where children dress up as white and black pieces on a giant board and take part in a game directed by two players). Older children, again, could help to make their own costumes. There are so many aspects of chess which can be used in these subjects: paint pictures or make collages based on chess themes:

use the chessboard and pieces to help understand and demonstrate perspective: photography of chess players and chess pieces. Just let your imagination run riot.

History

Most children of junior school age love hearing stories of battles, and, as we've seen, this is exactly what chess is. You can use children's interest in knights and castles, kings and queens, to introduce them to military history through the ages. Look at the history of chess through the Middle Ages, and see how the game spread westward from Asia to Europe along the trade routes. Older children might want to look at the history of modern tournament chess, going back to the first modern international match in 1834 and the first international tournament in 1851, learning about the great players of the past and looking at their games. There are many other great games children can enjoy playing, but only chess offers this extraordinary heritage.

Geography

Where there's history there's also geography. As well as looking at all the history connected with chess you can look at a map and see for yourself where it took place. Lots of chess openings are named after places, countries or sometimes towns, in one famous case, an island: can you find them on a map? If you're following international chess (you should if you're ambitious), what countries do the top players come from? What countries are the best in the world? Why do you think that is? Where are the tournaments taking place?

Modern Languages

If your children are learning a foreign language, or if they're bilingual, they should learn the names of the chess pieces and other chess terms (check, checkmate, stalemate, draw) in the language they're learning. Some children might be interested in learning these in a number of languages. What happens when you translate the words back into English? Are they the same? If not, why not? Why do you think some chess pieces have very different names in different countries? If you go on holiday, take a chess set with you. You might have the chance to practise French or Spanish at the same time as practising your chess.

Science

The links with science may be less obvious than with other subjects but there's still much you can do. What are your chess pieces made from? How are they made? What other materials can be used to make chess pieces? What are the advantages and disadvantages of each? Maybe you've got a magnetic chess set. How does this work? Children taking part in tournaments will be familiar with chess clocks (timers). There are two types: digital and analogue. How do they work? Why do they have two faces? What's the difference between the two types? Children are often amazed when they see me wind up an analogue clock.

ICT

Chess and computing are natural bedfellows: interest in both subjects tends to go together: and playing chess on the computer is much more useful than the many other time-wasting games you can play. Children could use their interest in chess to develop their internet researching skills. They could even design and program a simple website about chess: more advanced players could use this to demonstrate their own games. Of course there are many sites where you can play chess (in real time or turn-based), learn chess, practise solving puzzles, find out about chess news, consult online databases and much else. There's much more of this in the Resources chapter.

11

FINDING A CHESS TEACHER

Whether you're a parent or a teacher, you might consider hiring a professional chess teacher for your child or school. What should you be looking for?

First of all you'd be looking for someone who's passionate about chess, passionate about teaching, and who is able to communicate both with children and with parents and teachers. There are a lot of great teachers out there, but there are also some who have no particular interest in the process of teaching, but are doing it purely as a business, or to supplement their income from playing. There are some who choose the job of a chess teacher because they are passionate about both chess and teaching, even though they could earn more money by doing something else, while there are others who choose the job because they are unable or unwilling to do anything else. Schools, of course, are legally required to ensure that any teacher they use has gone through the appropriate checking procedures. If you're a parent you might want to ask to see a potential teacher's DBS/CRB certificate. You might also want to ask for references. There are some teachers out there who make misleading claims as to their chess strength and give misleading advice to their students. Anyone who has played competitive chess at any time will have had a grade (England) and/or rating (international or most other countries). These can be checked out, going back a number of years, on the internet. If you're looking for a teacher for your school club, would you appoint this person to teach any other subject, assuming they had the appropriate knowledge and qualifications? If you're considering using a private tutor, is this person so passionate about teaching chess that he/she would pay you for the privilege of teaching your children?

Class teachers and private tutors require very different skill sets. Class teachers need to be able to control a class and hold the attention of a large number of children at the same time. They need to be performers, actors. Private tutors need to be able to tune in to their students' wavelength, to give them the time, space and confidence to express their thoughts and feelings. If you like, a class teacher should be a good speaker, while a private tutor should be a good listener. Some teachers can do both, others will have a preference.

Again, teaching younger, less experienced children and teaching junior internationals require different skills. If you're teaching very strong players you need to be a very strong and knowledgeable player yourself. If you're teaching younger novices, which is what this book is mostly about, you don't need to be a strong player (although you do have to be aware of your limitations), but you do need some understanding of how children think and process information. At this level children need very little technical chess knowledge: instead they need to develop the learning skills necessary to process technical information accurately. A lot of teachers who are brilliant at higher levels are unaware of this and give young children too much technical knowledge too quickly without checking that it has really been understood rather than just half remembered.

Different teachers will have had different past experiences and will have different expectations. There are some things you need to check first to avoid possible misunderstandings.

If you're looking for a teacher for a school chess club, you'll need to agree financial terms and how your teacher expects to be paid. In some cases the parents will pay the teacher directly, either once a term or once a week. Other teachers prefer to be paid by the school on a termly basis. Some schools will insist on having at least one member of staff or parent in the room while the club is in progress, while other schools will leave the teacher alone to get on with it. Some teachers will prefer to have someone else in the room to keep order while they concentrate on teaching, while others will object, not wanting to feel that they are being watched all the time. You might want to agree on whether you expect the teacher to be teaching all the time (which may be what you want if the children are playing chess every day) or just to give a short lesson and spend the rest of the time watching them play (which will be desirable if children are only playing once a week). You might want to agree on whether the children should address the teacher by his/her first name or as Mr/Miss. The teacher might on occasion want to contact parents directly: how should this be done, given that many schools will not release contact details to outsiders? You might want to agree on whether your school should participate in the UK Chess Challenge, or play matches against other schools. You might want to ask whether he/she uses a set curriculum or prefers to relate the lessons to what happens in the children's games. It's as well to discuss these issues in advance so that you both know what to expect.

If you're looking for a private tutor for your children, you'll have a different set of questions. In a sense, you are your children's best teacher. You understand them better than anyone else. Teach them the basics, and, if they show a real passion for the game along with a competitive spirit, then you might think about hiring a private tutor. I've wasted a lot of time over the years visiting families who use me to teach the basics because they don't have time themselves. If your children are only doing chess once a week, whether at home or at school, and nothing is being reinforced between your teacher's visits, they will make no progress. You'll find that stronger players (particularly

Grandmasters and International Masters) often charge much more than other teachers. Some of them are excellent at working with younger children, but others are much more suited to higher level tuition. You'll be looking first of all for someone with experience with, and a particular understanding of, less experienced players. Some teachers will be prepared to travel to you (but will charge more for doing so) while others, maybe those who don't have their own transport, will prefer you to come to them. You might want to be in the same room so that you can see what's happening in the lesson, learn from it yourself and learn how to help your children better, or you may prefer to listen out of sight in the next room. Some tutors may not want you in the same room, as the children and the teacher might both feel restricted in what they can say in the presence of a parent. Other tutors might prefer you to be there as long as you don't interfere in the lesson too much. I've had pupils in the past where I've ended up teaching the parents rather than the children. You might want to agree on whether or not your children should be given homework, and, if so, what form it should take and how much time should be expended on it. If your children are passionate about chess and their tutor is passionate about teaching, their chess lesson should be one of the highlights of their week.

12

PLAYING CHESS
WITH YOUR KIDS

If you're reading this book I trust you're going to want to play chess with your children. Indeed, if you want your children to do well at chess it's vital that you do so. If you get it right you'll help them enormously, and enjoy the process yourself as well. If you get it wrong, you could easily put them off chess for life.

What you don't do is teach your children the moves in ten minutes, play some games against them and beat them every time. What you also don't do is play badly against them: they will develop bad habits which will be hard to get rid of. Ideally, you'll already at least know what good chess looks like before starting to play your children, or at least be prepared to learn with them. You, as an adult, will probably find it much easier than your children to understand the logic, strategy and tactics of the game. According to the celebrated American chess teacher David MacEnulty, an adult can learn in half an hour what a first grader will learn in six hours. If you find a concept difficult, your children will find it much more difficult.

'Talking through' your games with your children as you play them is an immensely powerful teaching and learning tool. This involves Socratic questioning concerning the game: asking or explaining why you played your moves and asking why your children played their moves. By doing this you'll be able to reinforce good moves and good thinking habits while identifying and gently correcting bad moves and bad habits.

We can identify three phases of chess development. The first stage is vision, learning to look at the chessboard, see at a glance where every piece is and what it can do next, and learning to check your move to see that it's safe and thus avoid one-move blunders. The second stage is calculation, learning to develop depth of thought by looking ahead and analysing forcing variations, and learning to develop breadth of thought by considering more (or better) alternatives. The final phase is judgement, working out how to assess positions above and beyond a simple count of material, learning about positional factors: mobility, king safety, pawn formation, the difference between bishops and knights, and long-term planning, understanding the concept of compensation (the balance between material and positional factors).

For the first year or two children will mostly be learning chessboard vision (although if you follow the sequential course outlined later in this book, you'll get an early opportunity to look at some very simple calculation) so your questioning at this stage will focus mainly on what your children can see on the board.

Young children enjoy winning games, and the more quickly and easily they win the more they like it, so it's a good idea, especially with very young beginners, to start with positions where they have a very large advantage. If you're playing a complete game for the first time, you could even start with just king and pawns against all their pieces. If you've gone through the mini-games first you might want to give yourself, for instance, a bishop and knight, as well. Children often like to be able to decide for themselves which pieces you should start with. Some children, on the other hand, will insist that you start with all your pieces. With older children (age 8 or 9 upwards) it's usually better to start playing complete games straight away as they'll be able to understand why they lose.

Suppose you make a move which threatens an enemy piece. Don't say anything at first but see how they respond. If they make a move to meet your threat say something like 'Well spotted! You saw that I was threatening your queen!' Use praise liberally, but always specifically: don't just tell them they played a good move but reinforce what was good about it. If they're hesitating you could ask 'Do you see what I'm trying to do next?'. If they play a move which fails to meet your threat you could let them take the move back and ask them to think again about your threat. If they make a threat, comment on it and praise them for doing so. Likewise, if they make a move which develops a piece, puts a piece on a better square, attempts an exchange or serves any other useful purpose, comment and praise. If they play an apparently pointless move, ask why they played it. They might say something like 'because it's safe', which isn't a good reason (although 'because it's unsafe' is a good reason not to play a move), in which case you might ask them to suggest a more useful move. They might also say 'I've got a plan but I'm not going to tell you what it is', which usually means that they haven't got a plan at all.

Encourage aggressive moves and moves that try to exchange pieces. Chess is war – you have to kill the soldiers in the other guy's army and it's inevitable that some of your soldiers will lose their lives in the process. If you don't attack you won't win. Children are quite right to be concerned about making sure their pieces are safe but the way to do this is to look at the board and see for yourself what is and isn't safe, not to keep them all in the corner because they might not be safe out in the open.

Throughout the game, throw in other questions like 'How many different checks could you play?', 'How many captures could you make?', 'How many queen moves do you have?', 'How many safe queen moves do you have?'.

Once your children have developed their chessboard vision to the point where they are usually avoiding one-move blunders you'll start asking a different set of questions based on developing the skill of calculation. This involves decision making and looking ahead, which many children find difficult. If children look ahead at all it's more 'I go there, then I go there, then I go there' rather than 'I go there, then you go there, then I go there'.

Your questions will help to develop depth of vision: 'What do you think is going to happen next?', 'What do you think my next move is going to be? What will you do after that?', and to develop breadth of vision: 'What other moves did you consider before you played that move?', 'Why didn't you move to that square instead?', 'Why didn't you move your knight instead?'. This is very hard for young children, who will tend to select one criterion for their move and play the first safe move that fulfils that criterion. Considering several criteria and several moves which meet those criteria, and then making a rational choice based on dynamic considerations involves advanced complex logic, which is exactly why chess is so difficult for many young children. Children will often reject a move which they don't like, and, without further thought, choose an alternative which may be far worse. They will often also select a move that sets a trap, but which allows their opponent to obtain a winning advantage by playing something else. Another common type of mistake is to play a move which looks good without stopping to check whether or not it really is safe.

At this point you can introduce the acronym CCTV: Checks, Captures, Threats and Violence (or, if you prefer, Checks, Captures and Threats lead to Victory). Your children can imagine using a closed circuit television camera to look at the board for forcing moves. We're using very different thinking skills in positions with and without forcing moves. Forcing moves: checks, captures and threats, require accurate calculation. In positions without forcing moves we're looking more at long-term plans: where do we want our pieces and how can we get them there? Asking children to talk to their pieces will get across the idea that they need to consider different moves.

If you're a good enough player to do so, explain from time to time (not necessarily every move) why you played the move and what you think is going to happen next. You can do this in a deliberately vague way ('If you go there then I'll go there and it's checkmate') to encourage them to work out for themselves what you're thinking about, and, if necessary, give them clues.

One thing to be careful about, especially if you're a strong player yourself, is your choice of vocabulary. As explained elsewhere, it helps to be very precise about the definitions of the terms 'attack' and 'threat'. We also talk very much in abstract terms about chess moves and positions, using words which we might assume children will understand, but, when we question them (as we should) we may well find they don't understand what we're talking about. I find, for instance, that if I describe a move as being 'passive' they have no idea what I mean so I have to explain it. As your children make progress and get beyond the idea of thinking purely in terms of points they'll meet the concept of 'compensation', where one player gives up material to get a strong position. When I ask, I find children often say they haven't heard the word 'compensation', or they define 'condensation' instead! So: be precise about your chess vocabulary, and, if you need to use a difficult or abstract word make sure your students know what it means.

Talking through a game works in three ways: the children receive positive reinforcement when they play a good move and constructive advice when they don't, while at the same time developing their verbalisation skills: putting their thoughts into words. At the same time, by listening to what you're saying and how you're describing your moves they learn how to play at your level rather than their level.

13

SOLVING CHESS PUZZLES
WITH YOUR KIDS

Besides playing games, children should also spend time solving chess puzzles on a regular basis. While there are many sources of puzzles suitable for children who have developed 20-20 chessboard vision, understand the fundamental logic of the game and are able to look ahead, there are not many sources of puzzles for novices. At this level children need one-move puzzles designed to reinforce basic concepts and develop sight of the board. Books that come with cartoons and kid-friendly titles might look attractive, but they are usually much too advanced for beginners: you'll need to look for formal courses or software written by chess education specialists to find what you're looking for. The Resources chapter will point you in the right direction.

So, having found some suitable puzzles, how should they be approached? There are three methods: setting the position up on the board, solving from a book or worksheet or solving on a computer screen. They all have their advantages and disadvantages, and more experienced solvers will have their own personal preferences.

With young beginners, though, you should start by setting the position up on the board and getting your children to solve the puzzle in front of them. Firstly, it's on a real board: looking at a two-dimensional representation of a board in either a horizontal (book or worksheet) or vertical (screen) plane is not the same thing at all. Using a real board will probably make the puzzles easier to solve: they won't be confused about which is the king and which the queen, and it will be easier for them to remember the patterns and use them in their own games. They will also get personalised feedback from you rather than just being told whether they're right or wrong. Firstly, you have to make sure you set the position up correctly (it's very easy to miss off a piece, put it on the wrong square or fail to remove a piece from the previous question, especially if you're doing it upside down) and ensure that the children know whose move it is (they should be facing the side to move) and exactly what they have to do. Encourage them to work out the answer for themselves rather than guess. Suppose, for example, you're doing Mate in 1 puzzles. When they give you an answer (which they will often do as a question – 'Is it this move?'), don't just tell them it's right or wrong. Instead, ask them why. To solve a Mate in 1 you need to ask yourself four questions. Is it check? Can he move to a safe square? Can he block the check? Can he capture the checking piece? If your answers are Yes, No, No, No, then you've solved the puzzle. Get your children to go through this process themselves until they are confident that they can get the right answer for the right reason. All the time you're asking yourself what they're thinking about, what they're seeing on the board, whether they really understand what they're doing. Are they seeing all the pieces or missing something on the other side of the board? Have they really grasped the concept of checkmate? There's no way they'll get this sort of feedback, or, indeed, that you will get this sort of understanding of them, by just giving them a worksheet to do.

Once children are confident and fluent at a particular question type, then you can move onto worksheets, or give them a chess puzzle book. You'll need to have the answers available so that you can mark them yourself. (Alternatively, of course, your chess teacher or tutor will have set the homework and will be able to mark them.) If they make a mistake, ask them if they can work out why the answer is wrong. Set the position up on a board for them if necessary. If they get stuck on a question, encourage them to set the position up and move the pieces round if they need to do so. For questions such as Mate in 1, children will have the choice of writing down their answer in notation or indicating the move by drawing an arrow on the diagram. Younger children will usually prefer the arrow but it's a good idea to encourage children to use notation as soon as they're ready. Getting used to notation is an important skill which will help them when reading chess books or recording their own games and one way of helping them with this is to encourage its use when solving puzzles.

There are two problems that children have with worksheets (not just chess worksheets). The first is that they often fail to read the instructions, or fail to notice when the instructions have changed, so often do completely the wrong thing, such as answering the question for Black instead of White. The second is that when they get stuck on a question they often give up completely rather than moving onto the next question. Eliminating these two issues will help children with their schoolwork as well as with their chess. It's because of these problems that worksheets may not be suitable for very young children.

The third method of solving puzzles is via a computer: either software or through a website. This is more suitable for older children who are able to work out for themselves why an answer is wrong without help from a parent or teacher. The advantages are that you get immediate feedback as to whether you're right or wrong, you don't have to stop and set up the position, and your eyes are not distracted by the other diagrams on the page. In addition, many children prefer screen-based learning to pencil and paper. The Resources chapter offers a selection of appropriate websites and software.

14

USING *CHESS FOR KIDS* AND CHESSKIDS ACADEMY

Chess for Kids is not like most chess books for children. The concept of 'Teach Yourself Chess' for seven-year-olds is meaningless: chess is far too complicated for children to teach themselves at that age. So I decided to write a story book, with cartoons and humour, instead.

The book can be read on several levels. Firstly, most children enjoy reading it simply as a story book, which is fine in itself but they won't learn a lot about chess in that way.

Then, it can be used as a manual for learning the moves of the pieces along with simple tactics and strategy. To do this effectively, you'll need to use a chessboard while reading the book, play through the moves of the games Sam and Alice play while learning chess, and discuss them with your children.

In the book, Sam and Alice not only have to learn about chess: they also have to learn a whole host of cognitive and noncognitive skills in order to put what they've learnt into practice. Sam has to learn how to control his impulses, how to listen to others and make decisions based on their views, how to develop the mental toughness required not to give up when things start going wrong or becoming too hard for him. Alice has to learn to be more aggressive, more decisive and more self-confident.

The book also provides opportunities for parents and teachers to discuss with their children subjects like the difference between typical boys and typical girls, the nature of aggression, violence and war, how to deal with bullying, what is the nature of courage, what makes someone a hero.

My free chess teaching website chessKIDS academy (the 'straight' version is at www.chesskids.org.uk and the humorous version at www.chesskids.me.uk) offers a wide range of coaching materials and advice for parents and teachers. The original concept was a course taking children from learning the moves through to adult club standard, comprising a series of short interactive lessons followed by a quiz to test and reinforce their knowledge. If you get all the questions right in the quizzes you can print out a certificate with your name on it. The elementary parts of the course, those which teach vision rather than calculation and judgement, can be accessed from the front page via the left-hand menu. The Intermediate Lessons tab will take you on to the next stage.

But this in itself was not enough. Different children learn best through different media, so I commissioned Peter Lalic, now an aspiring chess teacher himself, to produce short videos for the elementary lessons. Children who prefer to learn through books can, of course, follow the same material through *Chess for Kids*.

Children also need to play chess, so there are several chess computers available, three of which are suitable for beginners and novices. There are two relatively weak programs, both written in JavaScript and available in the public domain (one is no longer supported), which have been debugged and tweaked so that you can print out the moves of your games and study them afterwards. They have also been set to play on ten levels based on material. On level 1 you get all your pieces while the computer only has king and pawns. Gradually the computer starts with more pieces until level 10 where it plays with a full set. If your children decide they want to become serious competitive players, they will need to go through every game they play in order to improve, but it's not a bad idea to start now. There's also a Java program in the public domain (Little Chess Partner), a much stronger player, which has been programmed to give odds in the same way.

What you can do is to set up a chart with these three computer programs and the ten levels, and fill in the date when your children beat each program at each level. This will encourage them to move up and set themselves new challenges rather than just repeating what they can already achieve. At the lower levels you can win quickly, especially against the two weaker programs, by just bringing your queen out and capturing pawns. If your children are doing well they'll be able to beat the program we call Kaspy at level 10 within a year or so. It makes one-move blunders, so if you can avoid doing so you'll win. The other JavaScript program, Fishy, is slightly harder to beat, but still makes some elementary mistakes and shouldn't take too much longer to vanquish. The third program (Deep Red on the website) is a very different proposition, playing to the level of a strong adult club player.

Some children may have problems defeating the programs even on the lowest levels. This is because they fail to look at what the computer is doing against them. The programs move quickly and you might not notice what they've done, but you still have to learn to look at your opponent's checks, captures and threats. The other problem children will have is that they find they can't make the move they want to play. This is almost always because they haven't noticed that they're in check, so you'll have to intervene and help them. Another thing to note is that with all these programs you castle by playing the king move: the computer will move the rook for you automatically.

One of the programs has also been set to play some of the mini-games in the early part of the course. If you're using the humorous version of the site you'll note that he is an unsporting opponent: this is designed partly to make children laugh and partly to enable parents and teachers to talk to their children about what constitutes good sportsmanship. There is quite a lot of this sort of subversive humour at various points in this version of the site as well as in *Chess for Kids*.

You also have the option of printing off the moves of any games you play against Kaspy or Fishy. (Note that, at the time of writing, they use 'computer notation', giving the starting and finishing squares but not the identity of the piece.) It's an excellent idea to take advantage of this: to print off any games your children play and go through them together, discussing the moves that were played by both sides.

Young children should always be supervised when using chessKIDS academy and other online learning sites. They need adult supervision to enable them to pace themselves through the course: so that they won't continue repeating an easy task (such as beating the computers at a low level) and at the same time they won't tackle material which is too hard for them. So if you want your children to use this or any other similar site it would help if you could familiarise yourself with what's available first.

15

CHESSBOARD ETIQUETTE AND SPORTSMANSHIP

Chess may be a game with a strong undercurrent of violence but it is, or should be, played in a sportsmanlike way within a strict code of etiquette.

Children playing chess, especially at school, need first of all to learn how to look after their equipment. Chess should not be seen as a children's game and chess sets should not be seen or treated as toys. This means that children should be expected to treat the equipment with respect. Throwing or banging pieces should be strictly forbidden within a chess club. If you knock a piece on the floor you should pick it up straight away, and certainly not replace it with a piece from someone else's set. When you've finished a game of chess you should set up the pieces for a new game, even if it's the last game you're going to play. (Children never seem to understand the reason for this and look confused when you ask them to set up the pieces after their last game.) Children should be encouraged not to put their pieces back into the box unless they are certain they have a complete set. An alternative is to pair the pieces off, white and black, as you put them back into the box. If you're using roll-up boards they should be stored flat rather than rolled-up as they will become creased if they are not used for a week. If you have chess clocks (which most schools won't really need) they should be treated with extreme care.

It's because pieces can so easily get lost or broken that many schools are reluctant to let children play chess outside the weekly club, but if you teach your children these rules, and ensure that teachers who might be supervising their use are also aware, there's no reason not to encourage children to play at break or lunchtime should they wish to do so.

Serious chess competitions inevitably take place in silence. 'Tournament conditions' means exactly the same thing as 'exam conditions'. It's not realistic to enforce this in most primary school chess clubs: some children are not confident about the rules, and many of the children just want to enjoy playing with their friends and not take things too seriously, but voices should be kept down to a whisper and children should raise their hand if they have a problem.

In a tournament, you're expected to introduce yourself at the start of the game if you're playing someone you don't know, shake hands and wish each other good luck. At the end of the game you shake hands again. If you win you may say something like 'Bad luck. You played well', or, if you lose, 'Well played. I enjoyed the game', or words to that effect. Children should really be taught at home to 'win with grace and lose with dignity' but sometimes they have to learn these lessons at school. In any case, they should learn them before taking part in outside tournaments or matches.

You might want to introduce this within a school chess club, or you might prefer to be less formal but explain it to your children before they play in a competition or a match against another school. If you're playing a match against another school it's a good idea to get everyone to shake hands with their opponent before the start of the game.

You might also want to introduce the 'touch and move' rule within the club. There's more about this later on but, in brief, if you touch a piece with the intention of moving it you must do so if you can, and if you touch an enemy piece (with your hand or your piece) with the intention of taking it, again you must do so. I prefer not to insist on this for complete beginners but to introduce it once they can play fluently (some of them will have learnt it at home anyway).

16

WHAT YOUR KIDS NEED BEFORE STARTING CHESS

1. Motor Skills

Picking up the pieces and placing them in the centre of squares is not so easy for young children. Making captures – picking up your piece, removing the enemy piece from its square and replacing it with your piece – is something many young children find very difficult. They will often get confused and place the capturing piece on a different square or leave the captured piece somewhere else on the board.

2. Hand-eye-brain Coordination

Young children often have difficulty following lines of squares diagonally, or even vertically and horizontally. If they want to move a rook from, say, a2 to g2, it will often end up on g3 instead.

3. Game Playing Skills

I sometimes find myself having to teach young children who find it hard to take it in turns to move, who are unable to remember whose turn it is to move, and who are unable to play without cheating, not because of any malevolent intent but because they are unaware of the idea that games have rules which you have to follow. These skills should be taught at home using simple turn-taking games before children learn to play complete games of chess and join a chess club.

4. Short-term Memory

Young children will often forget what they have just been told. They may also forget where their pieces are on the board. If they knock a piece over, which often happens if their motor skills are not fully developed, they will usually replace it on a random square, perhaps because they can't remember where it was, or perhaps because they think it doesn't matter as long as it's somewhere on the board. They will sometimes replace a captured piece somewhere on the board, or remove a piece that's on the board, thinking it's been captured.

5. Long-term Memory

Children who are only doing chess once a week at school will often forget what they've been taught if it is not reinforced daily at home. Young children will often forget something even from one day to the next, especially if it is something abstract rather than concrete.

6. Working Memory

Recent research suggests that working memory is one of the most important factors in academic success. It's certainly true of chess. If you're talking through a game with your children you'll be giving them a lot of information which they need to hold in their memory. A typical mistake is that your opponent creates a threat. You decide to check him and deal with the threat later on. By the time it's your move again you've totally forgotten about the original threat.

7. Logic

Chess is essentially a logical game, which is why I see little point in doing too much before children reach the concrete operational stage of development. There is an underlying logic: if you threaten my queen I must do something about it because I don't want to lose my most powerful piece. You might assume that children make mistakes because they don't see things, but if you ask them you'll often find that they saw it but failed to apply the logic of chess correctly.

If you like you can use activities with the simpler pieces (rooks and bishops) to develop some of these skills, but there are many other board and strategy games that can be used as well.

17

WHAT YOU NEED BEFORE STARTING TEACHING CHESS

1. A Chess Set

It might seem obvious but you'd be amazed at how many children in school chess clubs tell me they don't have a chess set at home. But not just any chess set will do. Chess is very much about visual memory and pattern recognition: you might recognise a position on one set but it will look very different on another. Whatever you do, don't play on a Harry Potter, Simpsons, Star Wars or Lord of the Rings set. If you're a fan it's great to have them in the house but you really shouldn't use them to play chess: you'll only get confused. That lovely glass or marble chess set you bought on holiday might look beautiful but again it's best not to use it for serious games or training. The chess sets you can buy in the high street or on Amazon are better, but still not ideal. You really need to order from a specialist chess retailer. If you're within reach of central London there's a chess shop there, or there might be an equipment stall at a chess tournament in your area, but otherwise you'll need to buy over the internet. You're going to need a plastic chess set with 95mm king height. You'll also need a semi-rigid roll-up or folding chessboard with 50mm squares. These are what you'll use in tournaments and probably also in your school chess club (if they don't, tell them they should!). If you're using a roll-up board don't forget to store it flat, otherwise it will get creased. Wooden sets are also great, but more expensive, and most wooden boards don't have the coordinates round the sides – which you will need.

2. Furniture

Again something that may seem obvious but schools in particular often get this wrong. First of all, the two players should be sitting opposite each other, not next to each other or at right angles to each other. School chess clubs often take place in classrooms where children usually sit round large tables. This is really not suitable: you need to be facing your opponent in order to play your best. The table should not be so large that short arms have difficulty reaching to the end of the board to promote a pawn. It should also not be so small that there is nowhere to put all the enemy pieces you've captured. Children should be encouraged to place captured pieces at the side of the board (children who place pieces in front of them often think they should be on the board and try to replace them) and should be encouraged not to fiddle with them: this is potentially distracting both for them and for their opponent. Another point: chess teachers should, for obvious reasons, sit opposite rather than next to the child(ren) they're teaching.

3. Internet Access

The methods recommended in this book are based largely on my website www.chesskids.org.uk: everything on there is free for you to use. It's well worth spending a few hours going through everything on the site (in particular the Articles page) and seeing exactly what's available before starting to teach your children.

4. Books

You'll find a list of recommended books in the Resources chapter of this book. Most children will enjoy reading, or at least looking at, chess books. But be careful: many books which are marketed as being suitable for young children are actually adult books with added cartoons. Some of them are excellent books, but children often need two or three years' experience before they are ready for them. If you'll forgive the shameless plug, your children might enjoy reading my book *Chess for Kids*, which is essentially the companion book to the one you're reading now. You'll also need a supply of quizzes and worksheets, which you can find online (look out for my course *Journey Through Chess*) or from the books recommended in the Resources chapter. It includes a list of recommended books for parents, which will help them understand more about chess and how to help their children.

5. Chess Knowledge

You don't have to be a strong player yourself to help your children (in some ways it can be a disadvantage as strong players tend to go too fast for young children) but it does help a lot if you know what good chess looks like. You do have to know the rules of chess, though. Are you sure you can explain the *en passant* rule? If you haven't already done so, read Chapters 20 and 21, The Rules of Chess and Winning at Chess. At any rate you do need to keep one step ahead of your children. If you're giving them a lesson make sure you understand it fully yourself first. If you're giving them a worksheet make sure you know the correct answers, why they're correct and why other answers are incorrect. If you're going through an interactive lesson on chessKIDS academy with them, go through it yourself first, making sure you understand it and can answer all the quiz questions correctly.

6. Time

Perhaps the main theme of this book is that there's little point in signing your children up for a chess club at school unless you have the time to help them. Children who are not getting help at home will enjoy chess for a year or so, but they will neither become strong players nor gain very much academic benefit from the game. Of course most children will just be happy playing casual games with their friends, but even so it's well worth spending a year studying chess regularly at home just to see whether or not chess is for them. I would see it very much in the same way as learning the piano. If your children have piano lessons, their teacher will expect them to practise for ten minutes or so every day. If you want your children to benefit from chess they really need to do the same thing. For beginners and novices, the time should be spent on a combination of playing games and solving puzzles: maybe 50-50 but the exact proportion will depend on the child.

18

CHESS AND COGNITIVE SKILLS

It is the very complexity of chess that makes it such a powerful teaching and learning tool. By breaking chess down into its component parts we can identify the cognitive skills required for chess success. We can teach these skills using chess or in other ways, and our children can use their new-found skills both to play better chess and to improve their performance in other fields.

Young beginners choose their moves through a combination of random selection, personal preference (I'll move the knight because it's my favourite piece), impulse, emotion, anthropomorphism and magical thinking.

Instead we want them to develop visuospatial awareness, to use deductive and inductive reasoning, decision making and calculation to choose their moves.

Helping children to make this journey involves a mixture of playing and talking through games and solving simple puzzles.

Some of the definitions of thinking skills in this chapter are perhaps slightly different from the way they would be defined by philosophers and logicians but they're the closest you can get in terms of considering different types of chess thinking.

1. Chess and Visuospatial Awareness

The first skill children need to develop when they are learning the game is chessboard vision: the ability to see at a glance what every piece can do, in terms of both moves and captures. This skill is as fundamental to chess players as knowing your tables is to mathematicians. Children need to play regularly with the understanding that they have to look at the whole board to develop this skill.

We can teach this skill while children are playing games by asking them questions. How many checks do you have in this position? How many captures do you have? How many squares could your queen move to? How many of those squares are safe? How many different ways are there for you to get out of check? How many moves will it take you for your knight to get to e5? We can also use simple one-move puzzles which will test and reinforce this skill.

2. Chess and Pattern Recognition

Pattern recognition is in essence an extension of chessboard vision. Research has shown that strong chess players see pieces as 'chunks': particular recurring constellations of pieces along with the moves and plans associated with them. Young beginners will start to see 'chunks' as they progress: ideas such as Scholar's Mate and bank rank mates, for instance, along with typical endgame positions. Figures of up to 300,000 have been quoted for the number of 'chunks' recognised by master players.

Children can be questioned on their pattern recognition skills. Have you seen a position like this before? Do you remember what happened? Will that help you find the best move now? But the real development of this skill will come beyond the beginner stage.

Pattern recognition can also be developed by puzzle solving: repeated tactical ideas will eventually become familiar and opportunities will be recognised in their games.

3. Chess and Memory

Memory, in its various forms, plays a very important part in chess.

Beginners have to learn how the pieces move, along with other rules such as castling and *en passant*. They will then learn basic procedures such as mating with a king and queen. Here, we're linking up with pattern recognition. Those children who move into higher level competitive chess will have to learn (and, more importantly, understand) openings: sequences of moves from the starting position which have been worked out over decades, or even centuries. They will also learn middle-game strategies associated with typical pawn structures, and endgame techniques.

A strong visual memory for chess moves and positions is a very useful attribute. One way to develop this is to demonstrate a short game, explaining the reasons for the moves as you go along, and then ask the student to repeat the moves. Test whether the moves have been transferred into long-term memory by asking the student to repeat the game the following day. Once this skill has been mastered, gradually increase the length of the game. Through this technique, students will increase their understanding of chess through your descriptions of the reasons behind the moves as well as developing their visual memory for chess moves.

Some children enjoy playing blindfold games: the players are not actually blindfolded but call out the moves to each other using standard chess notation. Again, this can be a useful skill which will help improve their chess.

A good working memory is vital not just for chess but for academic success generally. There has been much research demonstrating correlation between working memory and ability to perform complex cognitive tasks. The chessboard is a big place and you often need to keep track of several different things at the same time. Children who display competence in simple positions often go to pieces in more complicated situations. There are a number of websites which provide free exercises for developing working memory.

Some children have problems with associative memory: they can remember names of openings and their moves, but are completely unable to remember which names go with which moves. Again, this is a skill which can be trained.

Children who like memorising facts might like to collect information on the names of famous players and great tournaments, just as children who enjoy football might collect information on their favourite sport.

4. Chess and Generalisation

One of the biggest problems in teaching chess is that young children find it difficult to move from the general to the specific and from the specific to the general.

You can teach a general principle such as 'don't bring your queen out too soon', which is excellent advice, but there are many exceptions where it is not just good but necessary to bring your queen out early. It's very easy to fixate on the rule and not consider the exceptions, or to contradict your teacher when he advises you to bring your queen out early in a specific position.

On the other hand, if you show children a move they should play in a particular position they will often play it in positions where it is not appropriate. To give a typical example, after the moves 1. e4 e5 2. Nf3 Nc6 3. Bc4 Nf6 you may teach your students to play 4. Ng5, which, in this specific position, is an excellent move. The problem is that they will try to 'chunk' the position, or remember the move but not the exact position, and play Ng5 in other, similar but not analogous, situations where it is not a good move at all.

This is precisely why much tuition aimed at younger players is misdirected and, while teaching them to play one particular position well, often leaves children confused.

5. Chess and Decision Making

In one sense chess could be said to be all about the art of decision making. Young children, by and large, are not given much chance to make decisions. It's much easier for us as parents and teachers to tell them what to do and use rewards and punishments to get children to do what we want.

There are two parts to making a decision: considering what your options are and deciding what will happen in each case.

Take a simple decision: what topping would you like on your pizza, or what flavour ice cream would you like? It's just a question of taste. There's no need to think ahead beyond 'I like this flavour' and 'I don't like that flavour so much'.

But there are other decisions – should I do my homework or play a computer game this evening? – where your decision is based on what is going to happen next rather than just what you like. In other words, it's a decision based on forward thinking, logic and understanding of how other people will react to your decision, rather than emotion, assuming you have the self-control to stop and make the decision in the first place.

Simpler strategy games, including the mini-games you'll learn in my chess course, only present the player with a relatively small number of choices. A complicated chess position, on the other hand, may offer you forty or more choices. While computers have no problem considering every possible move, humans can usually only consider three or four moves in depth. The trick is choosing the right moves to analyse.

To become a good chess player you have to develop both breadth and depth of vision, and that takes years of practice, involving playing games and solving puzzles.

But first you have to understand that chess is about decision making, and learn how to make decisions. Children will typically think of a move, usually the first move they find that meets the one criterion they're considering, and, if it's safe, play it. Teaching decision making in chess involves, at least in simple positions, persuading the student to consider all the moves that meet the selected criterion (all the ways to defend the threatened pawn, for example, or all the safe squares for the threatened queen) and then decide which move he prefers. Sometimes you'll have to consider multiple criteria and try to find moves that meet all of them at the same time, for instance finding a move which meets both your opponent's threats.

Appropriate questioning when playing through a game (What other moves did you consider? What do you think will happen next?) can train decision making. Children can also learn this skill by answering multiple choice questions where you have to choose from two, three or four alternatives and decide on the one you like best. Such questions are particularly suitable also for testing and developing defensive skills and avoidance of blunders: which of the choices is the only safe move or the only one that meets the opponent's threat? Unfortunately there are at present not many sources of questions of this nature suitable for younger players.

Give your children more opportunity to make their own decisions in life as well. Ask them: 'What are your choices?' and 'What do you think will happen next? Who will be affected by your choice?'

6. Chess and Differentiation

When making decisions we have to differentiate between moves. This is something children find difficult. If you ask children why they played one move rather than another, they will often give a reason which applies equally to both (or all) your suggestions. For an example, set up a position with a white king on e2, black pawn on e3 and black king on d4 and ask them to choose a move for White. Whichever move they suggest, they will probably say, when asked for a reason, that they chose the move so that they can capture the pawn if it advances to e2. This, of course, applies to all four legal moves so indicates a lack of differentiation skills. (In fact the correct answer is that you should move to e1: this move draws with best play while other moves lose with best play.)

One reason for this is to do with children's problems in considering more than one criterion at a time when choosing a move. Another reason, in this sort of position, is a 'theory of mind' problem: only considering the move you hope your opponent will play rather than thinking what his best move would be. This skill can be honed by constant questioning when 'talking through' a game and by solving multiple choice questions.

7. Chess and Prioritisation

We give children lots of information when we're teaching them chess. We teach them the value of the pieces but we also give them more general advice such as 'don't bring your queen out too soon' or 'doubled pawns (two pawns on the same file) are weak so you should avoid them'. What we often fail to do is explain the relative importance of the information we're giving them.

So what happens sometimes is that, for example, your bishop takes their knight, and their only recapture is with a pawn giving them doubled pawns. Sometimes they will refuse to recapture because they've been told to avoid doubled pawns. This is a basic misunderstanding of the SFW (Superior Force Wins) concept. Positional factors such as doubled pawns only come into play when children are able to conduct a game without making tactical oversights. Typically, a positional factor might be worth about a third or a half of a pawn. This is, more than anything else, a failure on the part of the teacher to explain relative values and enable the student to prioritise appropriately.

The chessboard is a big place and sometimes there's a lot going on, which leads to another prioritisation issue. This is again to do with the difficulty children have in considering more than one criterion. So they will often see the less important threat, or perhaps something that isn't really a threat at all, and meet that while missing the more important threat. This is a different issue: children tend to stop when they see something and react to that rather than looking round to see what else is happening. This is why the same children who can play a perfectly competent game as long as the position remains relatively simple flounder hopelessly in more complicated positions.

8. Chess and Deductive Reasoning

If you wanted to teach deductive reasoning you'd probably use Sudokus rather than chess, but you could argue that the underlying logic of the game (Superior Force Wins) lends itself to deductive reasoning. If you play a move that threatens to win material, I, following the SFW logic, must do something about it.

It's striking how often young children, when asked a question about chess, will give an illogical answer. If you ask beginners which colour they'd prefer they often choose black, and explain that they will copy you until you make a mistake and then take advantage of it. I suppose there's an element of logic in this, but it fails to take into account the fact that you can't copy a check, sometimes you can't copy a capture, and sometimes copying a capture would be unwise. I've even seen games starting 1. e4 e5 2. Qh5 Qh4.

If a student plays a move that loses material you might assume either that they didn't look, or that they looked but didn't see. If you ask them, though, they will often tell you they saw it but hoped their opponent wouldn't notice or thought it didn't matter. Even fairly experienced players will sometimes give up a bishop against me and, when I ask them, reply 'I know. I don't care. I often win when I'm a bishop down.' Yes, you may well win when a bishop down against weak players but it's unlikely to help when you're playing your chess teacher!

When playing a game, question reasons for moves where appropriate and check the logic. Praise logical moves. You might consider a forfeit for anyone who plays a move that loses material (there are some suggestions in *Chess for Kids*)!

9. Chess and Inductive Reasoning

Inductive reasoning is the ability to draw general conclusions from specific examples. This is again the problem mentioned earlier. Young children will find this difficult because they are unable to move from the specific to the general.

Typically, chess teachers will demonstrate a game played by a strong player to a group of students and expect them to draw conclusions from that game that will improve their own play. Older children can learn in this way, but younger children, by and large, cannot. Because of the game's complexity, young children need specific advice on how they can improve their own play. Bottom up teaching rather than top down teaching.

You see the same thing in reverse if you show them a position in which a player wins by playing a sacrifice. Children (and not just children) will often aim for a vaguely similar position and play the sacrifice without calculating whether or not it works in that position. Tactics training is necessary for chess improvement, but students need to be careful about being over-reliant on using inductive reasoning/pattern recognition as a short cut.

10. Chess and Analogical Reasoning

Experienced players are using analogies all the time when playing chess. Young children, though, often find it difficult to use simple analogies to solve puzzles. For example, if children can solve a simple Mate in 1 puzzle they cannot always understand that the checkmate will essentially be the same if we rotate the position by 90 or 180 degrees (as long as pawns are not involved). The best move in an ending will again be essentially the same (unless the side of the board is involved) if we move everything one square to the left or right. Such inferences by use of analogy may be obvious to older learners but are not always obvious to young beginners. You may need to repeat your example several times in different but analogous positions to make your point.

11. Chess and Theory of Mind

Theory of mind is the understanding that other people have beliefs, desires and intentions that are different from one's own.

You could also see the idea that other people will not necessarily react in the way you want them to as something similar. Failure to appreciate what your opponent might be thinking is one of the causes of illogical decisions in chess.

Young children are always keen to set traps because they hope their opponent will fall into them, or just to play moves based on what they hope their opponent will do next. The idea that their opponent will try to find the best move is something they find very hard to appreciate. When talking through a game you could ask 'What do you think I'm going to do next?' or 'What do you think I'm thinking about?' to try to get your students to think about the position from their opponent's perspective as well as their own.

Look for examples in real life: 'What will your sister think if you do that?' or 'What will your teacher say if you don't do your homework?' may help your children take someone else's perspective and help them make better decisions in life as well as in chess.

12. Chess and Verbalisation

When you ask children what move they'd play next or what they are thinking about they'll often point to the piece and the square, and gesticulate by waving their hands about. If you ask them to explain without using their hands they'll find this very difficult. If possible, try to get them out of this habit and instead to tell you in words what they want to play and why they want to play it. This is one reason why it's useful to teach children the names of the squares (and ensure that you start with the white pieces on the ranks numbered 1 and 2).

Chess players aren't allowed to wave their hands about when playing a competitive game. Learning to verbalise thoughts is an important skill which will help your children put their ideas in order and make better decisions over the board.

13. Chess and Scientific Method

Scientific Method is, in loose terms, the process of forming a hypothesis, testing it and either accepting or rejecting it.

This is something you don't very often do during a chess game but you certainly use this technique when solving tactics puzzles. The difference is that in a puzzle you often have a specific aim such as finding a Mate in 1 move. When solving such puzzles during a one-to-one lesson, children will usually make a guess and ask their teacher whether or not it's right. Instead, we can train them to ask themselves the same question. Is it check? Can he move his king? Can he interpose a piece? Can he capture the checking piece? If the answers are Yes, No, No and No, they can accept the hypothesis that their first guess is correct. If not, they have to guess a different move. They might be able to make a better guess by considering why their first guess didn't work. For instance, if the king can move to a safe square they'll have to find a different check that controls that square.

Once children master this technique they're using Scientific Method, and developing skills that can be applied in scientific study at school and in many other aspects of their lives.

This exercise can work very well within a group with children working in pairs. If they both agree on an answer they may well be right, but if they disagree they'll have to look again to see which answer is correct.

When students become proficient in Mate in 1 puzzles they can move on to Mate in 2 puzzles, followed by Mate in 3. Puzzles of this nature are available on chessKIDS academy.

14. Chess and Calculation

There is a strong correlation between chess and maths, both of which involve calculation. In fact it's often said that chess is 99 per cent tactics or 99 per cent calculation. There's an element of truth in that, but, as explained elsewhere, if you play better strategic chess, placing your pieces on more effective squares, the tactics are more likely to work in your favour.

What we mean by calculation in chess is very different from mathematical calculation, though. In its simplest terms, chess calculation is 'I go there, he goes there, I go there'. How, children often ask, are you supposed to know what he's going to do next? The answer is that we can only calculate meaningfully in this way in forcing positions. If we check, he has to get out of check. If we initiate an exchange, he may well take back. If we threaten his queen he'll probably move it. We can think in terms of a tree: each of his legal or reasonable choices is a different branch. Ideally we'll go down every branch until we reach a position where there are no more forcing moves, whereupon we'll assess the position at the end of each branch and make our decision accordingly.

To do this we need various skills: chessboard vision, to see all possible forcing moves, the ability to see 'in your head' the position as it develops over several moves, pattern recognition and inductive reasoning to identify position types we've seen before, and self-control to think through every possibility rather than rushing to play the first move that comes to mind.

Of course we develop these skills by attempting to calculate tactics during our games. We also hone our tactical skills by solving chess puzzles on a regular basis. Developing chessboard vision, and, later, visual memory, will also help.

15. Chess and Strategic Thinking

Parents often tell me they want their children to learn chess to improve their strategic thinking. I'm never quite sure what they mean by strategic thinking, though.

We can split chess into tactics (what to do when there's something to do) and strategy (what to do when there's nothing to do). The skill of calculation described in the previous section is essentially tactics. When there's nothing immediately happening tactically we think strategically.

We're talking here about long-term plans, about putting pieces on good (strong and safe) squares. But at lower levels games are decided tactically much more than strategically, and it's natural that if they can't make any immediate threats, children will choose a move which might enable them to play a threat next move. Learning genuine strategic thinking in chess requires maturity, experience, study and, most of all, inductive reasoning from the games you've studied, so that you can identify other games which reached similar positions and are aware of the plans that were chosen in those games.

16. Chess and Following an Algorithm

When you assemble a piece of flat pack furniture you're following an algorithm. When you're following a recipe to cook a meal you're following an algorithm. When you're writing a computer program you're teaching the computer to follow an algorithm. An algorithm is a multi-stage plan which is followed step by step.

Following an algorithm is what you're doing when you're learning how to checkmate with a king and queen against a king, or with a king and rook against a king. Children will learn these vital skills (although they might not realise it at the time) by following an algorithm.

It's a thinking skill which applies largely to endings of this nature in chess: learning the endings will help you win more games as well as learning a skill which has many applications in real life.

17. Chess and Brainstorming

Brainstorming is probably not something for beginners, but can be used as a teaching technique with, for instance, a small group of more advanced students. Give them a complicated position and ask them to come up with as many ideas as they can.

In our games we resort to brainstorming in positions where nothing obvious comes to mind, or where we're desperately looking for a way out of a difficult situation.

Although this is a thinking skill which will not be taught much to young beginners, it will certainly come in useful for anyone who wants to take the game seriously.

18. Chess and Critical Thinking

Critical thinking is, if you like, thinking about thinking, questioning your assumptions. If you threaten your opponent's queen he will probably have to move it – but he might possibly have something better. If you initiate an exchange he'll probably take back – but again he may have something better. An over-application of logic without applying critical thinking can often lead to mistakes.

Again, this is a difficult skill which will be used more by older players, but getting into the habit of thinking beyond the obvious, falsifying your intended move, asking yourself questions like 'If I play this move what could possibly go wrong?', 'What is the worst thing that could happen to me in this position?', 'Am I sure my assumptions are correct?' will be necessary in order to play chess to a high level. There has been some research which suggests that this particular skill of falsification is one of the factors that best differentiates between average and strong players.

19

CHESS AND NONCOGNITIVE SKILLS

1. Chess and Self-control

You're probably aware of the Stanford Marshmallow Test (1972) in which young children were given the choice between one marshmallow now or two in twenty minutes' time. Later follow-up research reported that the participants who were able to resist temptation would be more academically successful as teenagers and happier and more reliable as adults. The increasingly large number of children diagnosed with conditions such as ADHD suggests that more and more children have self-regulatory problems.

You need self-control in order to play chess well. Children without self-control will tend to play the first move that comes to mind without checking whether it's the best move, or whether or not it's safe. You might like to ask them what they do before crossing the road, and emphasise that they need to do exactly the same thing when they're playing chess.

The single biggest thing most beginners need to do to improve their chess is to stop and ask themselves 'Is it safe?' between thinking of a move and playing it. This requires a certain amount of self-discipline as well as the visual processing skill of being able to 'see' something that isn't actually in front of you. When playing training games against young children, remind them to stop and think each move: prompt them to ask the questions every move, 'What am I threatening?', 'What captures can I make?' and 'Is the move I want to play safe?' Eventually this will become second nature.

If children display a lack of self-control in other aspects of their life, you could use their interest in chess to remind them what happens if they play a move without thinking first.

2. Chess and Concentration

Chess is complicated. There's a lot going on that you have to think about. If you don't have 100 per cent concentration and focus you're not going to play well. A game of chess isn't worthwhile if you're thinking about your favourite football team or what you're going to have for dinner at the same time. You have to clear all the other junk out of your head before you start playing and focus on the chessboard and nothing other than the chessboard. You certainly can't play a worthwhile game of chess while chatting to your friend – and anyone else within earshot won't be able to play a worthwhile game either. This is why chess tournaments take place in silence – and if you're running a serious chess club it should also be silent.

Of course there's no reason why you shouldn't be able to play a non-serious game with your friend and chat at the same time. It will be enjoyable but you won't get a lot out of it. So school (and other) chess clubs have to decide whether they're a place for casual games or a place for serious games. You can't do both at once.

Children who enjoy chess and have strong powers of concentration are likely to do well in competitions and should be encouraged to study chess seriously. Children who enjoy chess but have problems with concentration and focus might like to use the game as a way to improve their concentration. Parents and teachers could work with children with this specifically in mind.

3. Chess and Perseverance

Chess, as we've seen, is a hard game. It's very easy for children to get stuck, lose interest and give up. One of the main problems with encouraging mass participation of young children is that they do indeed get stuck. This is one of the lessons Sam has to learn in *Chess for Kids* – not to give up when he doesn't understand something or keeps on making mistakes.

You can see this also when children are doing worksheets: if they hit a puzzle they can't solve they give up completely. Instead they could move onto the next question and come back later or set it up on a board and move the pieces round.

The ability to keep going when things get tough requires a certain emotional maturity that most young children don't have. They'll need your help, as parents and teachers, to encourage them not to give up but to learn to deal with this sort of situation.

4. Chess and Resilience

Taking the same idea a bit further, this applies particularly to those who play competitive chess. It happens to everyone: you play a bad game, you make a horrendous blunder and throw away a winning position. But you've got the next round coming up in ten minutes' time. Can you deal with it? Do you give up and go home? Do you play badly in your next game because you've lost your self-confidence? Or can you bounce back? Does your defeat make you more determined to play well, avoid mistakes and win next time round? Whatever doesn't kill you makes you stronger.

This is resilience: the ability to deal with the bad experiences that life, or chess, sometimes throws at us. Except that, with chess, but not always with life, you are the master of your own fate.

There are those who argue that young children shouldn't play competitive chess because they lack the emotional toughness to cope with bad experiences. They may well have a point, or you may decide that, as your children enjoy playing chess, you want to use competitive chess to help them develop the resilience that will help them with this and much else in their lives. As always, you know your children better than anyone else: it's your choice.

5. Chess and Optimism

If we're playing chess it helps a lot if we're optimistic: that our glass is half full rather than half empty. A feeling of confidence is important for us to play our best. Even if we're playing against a much stronger player, if we go into the game convinced that we don't stand a chance, that we'll lose whatever we do, then we almost certainly will lose. If, on the other hand, we go into the game thinking that if we play our best we stand a chance, that we start with an equal position and if we avoid mistakes we won't lose, then who knows what might happen? Likewise, if we find ourselves in a bad position we need to be optimistic that we can find a way out, or at least make things difficult for our opponent, rather than just assuming we're going to lose and switching off.

This is not the same as arrogance. If we're playing a much weaker player, or have a far superior position, we must avoid being overconfident. It's very dangerous to think 'I can beat this guy whatever I do' or 'My position's so good I can win without trying'. It's exactly in this situation that you have to be careful. Hubris, the Greeks called it. Dizziness due to success, say the Russians.

6. Chess and Courage

Because chess is an individual game, and a game of pure skill, if you take part in competitions you're very exposed. If you make a mistake it's your fault and your fault alone. You can't blame someone else for it. You can't say that you were unlucky.

It's the last round on the tournament. You're half a point behind the leader. If you beat him you'll win the tournament. Pressure. You're playing for your school or club in a match, perhaps a national championship. The scores are level with just your game to finish. It's a tense and exciting position with both players short of time. The other members of both teams are crowding the board watching you. Can you cope with it?

Contrary to popular opinion, chess is not a game for wimps. Competitive chess is very, very tough. To make the most of your ability you need grit, determination, courage. In other situations we might be called upon to demonstrate physical courage or moral courage. If you're playing competitive chess you might argue that you need mental courage in order to cope with the stress.

7. Chess and Self-esteem

Genuine self-esteem doesn't come from showering children with indiscriminate praise or from giving in to their every request. Instead it comes from knowing that you are good. Knowing that you are a good person, yes, but knowing that you're good at something also helps.

This means that we, as parents or teachers, should identify our children's passion and help them to run with it as far as they want to go. To enable them to be the best they can be within the time they have available.

Many children these days have so many interests that they are unable to excel at any of them. Parents sometimes tell me they only want their children to do chess for an hour a week because they want them to lead a balanced life. But, in everything they do, they compare themselves with children who are doing the same activity for five or ten hours a week and find themselves wanting. By the time they're 13 they're wandering round saying 'I'm stupid. I'm no good at anything.' Jack of all trades, master of none.

For many of us, our satisfaction in life comes from trying to excel at something that interests us. Your children might need to try lots of different activities before they find the two or three that they're really passionate about. Being able to follow, and perhaps excel at, your passion is what gives you genuine self-esteem.

The Hungarian-born psychologist Mihaly Csikszentmihalyi has popularised the concept of Flow: the idea that people achieve true happiness when they are totally immersed in an activity to the exclusion of everything else. The nature of chess makes it an ideal channel for achieving flow: but you need to get beyond the beginner stage of playing more or less random moves to attain this.

8. Chess and Self-motivation

One of the disadvantages of encouraging children to take part in competitive chess at an early age is that they need to be motivated. This means that you, their parents or teacher, have to motivate them to play and practise regularly, to solve puzzles on a daily basis, to attend chess clubs, to take part in competitions and so on. Some parents have the time to do this but others, often for the best of reasons, do not. This is one reason why I'd be cautious about encouraging children to take part in competitions if their parents are not able to support them in this way.

Eventually, though, children have to learn to motivate themselves, in chess and in life. When they're old enough (which would normally be around the age at which they start secondary school) you can help your children to motivate themselves to study, practise and play chess.

9. Chess and Self-criticism

This is another skill which children will really only develop at secondary school age, but it's a vital skill for all serious chess players.

If you ask young children why they lost a game they will almost certainly give you the wrong answer. They'll say 'I made a mistake and he mated me' when the real reason why they lost was that they lost their queen earlier in the game. You need intellectual maturity to identify, or try to identify, the tipping point in the game, and emotional maturity to do something about it. Did you make a tactical error? Were you outplayed strategically? Did your opponent know the opening better than you? Did you misplay the ending? Many chess players throw their scoresheet away in disgust when they lose a game. But that's not the way to improve. Anyone who is serious about chess will need to go through their losses with a stronger player and learn from their mistakes.

In time your children will learn to be self-critical, to work out for themselves what their mistakes were, and, more generally, to identify their strengths and weaknesses, and work on developing the former while ironing out the latter.

20

THE RULES OF CHESS

If you don't know how to play you need to read this. If you only play socially you should still read it: you may well find out a few things you didn't know. Many children in school chess clubs are not sure of all the rules – because their parents don't know all the rules either. You owe it to your children to make sure you get everything right before you start teaching them. If you're a serious competitive player you can skip this chapter.

1. The Chessboard

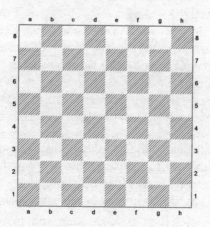

Fig. 1

The chessboard is made up of 64 contrasted light and dark squares arranged in 8 rows (ranks) and 8 files (files), as shown by Fig. 1. For notation purposes the squares are named by the letter of their file followed by the number of their rank: for instance a1, e4 or h8. We often refer to the light and dark squares as 'white squares' and 'black squares' regardless of their actual colour.

The board must be placed so that there is a light square in your right hand corner. If you are using a board with co-ordinates (which you should be) place the white pieces on the ranks numbered 1 and 2 and the black pieces on the ranks numbered 7 and 8.

Fig. 2

At the start of the game the board looks like Fig. 2. Rooks in the corners, knights next to the rooks, bishops next to the knights, queens on the d-file and kings on the e-file, with the pawns in front. The six different pieces all have their own way of moving.

The players take it in turns to move, with White making the first move. You can move a piece to a vacant square, or to a square occupied by an enemy piece, in which case you capture it by removing it from the board.

2. The Rook

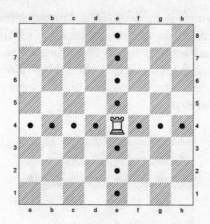

Fig. 3

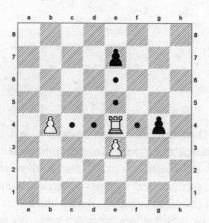

Fig. 4

Fig. 3 shows the rook move on an empty board. It can move as far as it likes in a straight line, vertically or horizontally. It's called a rook (from a Persian word for 'chariot'), by the way, NOT a castle. If you call it a castle in a chess club you'll be laughed out of court.

The rook cannot jump over pieces but can capture an enemy piece by moving to its square and taking it off the board. It is obstructed by a friendly piece. In Fig. 4 the rook can move to any of the marked squares or capture either black pawn.

3. The Bishop

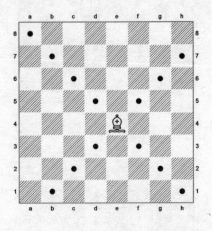

Fig. 5

Fig. 5 shows the bishop move on an empty board. It can move as far as it likes along a diagonal. Note that bishops can only move to squares of the same colour. If you find yourself with two bishops on the same colour square you've done something wrong (unless you've promoted a pawn to a bishop)!

Like the rook, the bishop cannot jump over pieces but can capture an enemy piece by moving to its square and taking it off the board. In Fig. 6 the bishop can move to any of the marked squares or capture either black pawn.

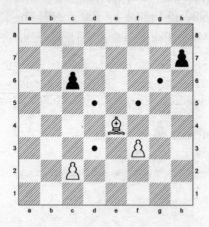

Fig. 6

4. The Queen

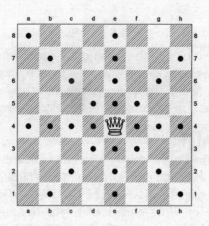

Fig. 7

Fig. 7 shows the queen move on an empty board. Its move is a combination of the rook move (horizontally or vertically) and the bishop move (diagonally). This makes it a strong piece: in fact it's the most powerful piece on the board. The king is the tall piece with the cross on top: the queen is the tall piece without the cross on top.

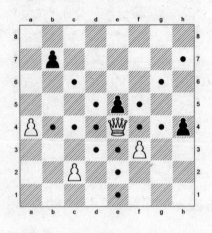

Fig. 8

Again like the rook and the bishop, the queen cannot jump but can capture an enemy piece by moving to its square and taking it off the board. Again, the queen can move to any of the marked squares on Fig. 8 or capture any of the black pawns.

5. The Knight

Fig. 9 shows the knight move on an empty board. The knight is very different from the pieces you've met so far and not easy for beginners to grasp. Its move can be considered a jump from one corner to the opposite corner of a 3x2 rectangle. It can be explained to children as a move in a letter L: two squares and then one round the corner. You can also define a knight as moving to the nearest non-adjacent square of the opposite colour. Unlike other pieces it can jump over any pieces (of either colour) in its way. Note that a knight on a light square always moves to a dark square and vice versa. It's always called a knight, certainly not a horse, still less a horsey.

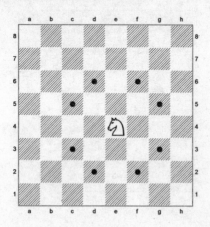

Fig. 9

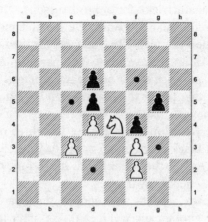

Fig. 10

In the position shown in Fig. 10 the knight can move to any of the marked squares or capture either of the black pawns on d6 or g5.

6. The Pawn

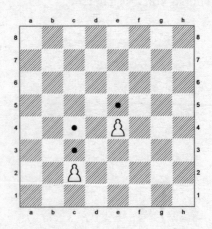

Fig. 11

The pawn is again tricky for several reasons. The basic pawn move is just one square forward. On its first move it has the additional option of moving two squares forward. In Fig. 11 the pawn on e4 can only move to e5. The pawn on c2 has not yet moved so may advance either one or two squares.

Unlike the other pieces the pawn does not capture in the same way that it moves. Instead it captures one square diagonally forwards. The pawn on b5 in Fig. 12 has three choices: it can capture either black pawn on a6 or c6, or it can advance to b6. The pawn on e4, on the other hand, has no moves at all. It is blocked by the enemy pawn on e5.

When a pawn reaches the end of the board it must be exchanged for another piece (Fig. 13). You have the choice of a queen, a rook, a bishop or a knight. Usually you'll choose a

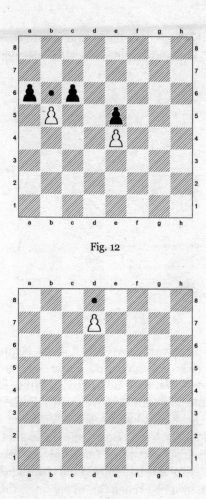

Fig. 12

Fig. 13

queen. This is called 'promoting a pawn'. The promoted piece starts on the promotion square, not on its starting square. Note that the promoted piece doesn't have to be a piece that was previously captured. You can have two, or in theory any number up to nine, queens at the same time, although two is usually enough! If you

111

don't have another queen available, you can, in casual games, use an upside down rook or two pawns together instead.

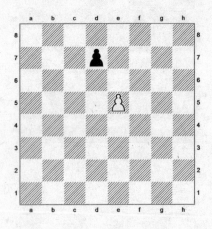

Fig. 14

There's one more pawn move which most beginners find the hardest rule in chess to understand. Some children play for years without fully understanding it. In Fig. 14 White has a pawn on his fifth rank. Black has an unmoved pawn on the next file.

It's Black's move and he chooses to advance his pawn two squares (Fig. 15). The 'en passant' rule states that White may if he chooses, on his next move (and only on his next move), capture the pawn as if it had moved only one square: while it is passing ('en passant' is French for 'in passing') the d6 square.

Fig. 16 shows the position after White has captured the black pawn en passant. Note that you can only make this move if (a) your pawn is on your 5th rank (rank no. 5 for White, rank no. 4 for Black) and (b) your opponent has, on his last move, moved a pawn on an immediately adjacent file two squares (not one square).

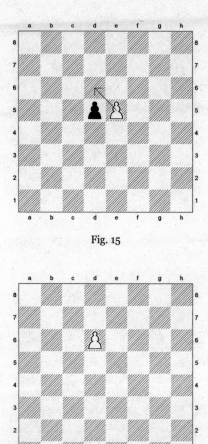

Fig. 15

Fig. 16

7. The King

Superficially, the king is the easiest piece to understand. This is all it does: it just moves – and captures – one square in any direction (Fig. 17).

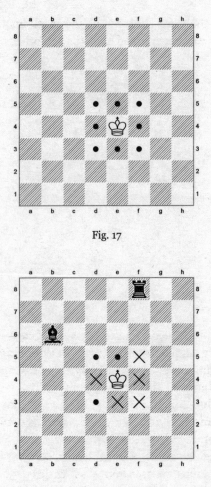

Fig. 17

Fig. 18

It's not quite as simple as that, though. You are not allowed to move your king to a square where it could be captured by another piece. In Fig. 18 the king can only move to the squares indicated by a circle. It cannot move onto the same file as the

114

black rook or the same diagonal as the black bishop. It follows that two kings can never stand next to each other.

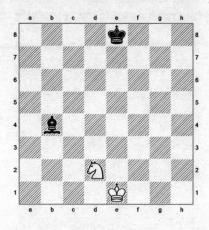

Fig. 19

You are also not allowed to make any move that leaves your king open to capture. In the position in Fig. 19 White is not allowed to move his knight because it would leave his king open to capture by the black bishop. This is called a pin. The black bishop is pinning the white knight.

Many children find it hard to understand the concept that you can never capture a king and at the same time you can never leave your king where it could (in theory) be captured.

If your opponent plays a move which leaves his king to be captured you must ask him to go back and play a legal move instead. You cannot claim a win by capturing the enemy king in this way.

8. Check
If you make a move which potentially leaves your opponent's king open to capture (attacks or threatens your opponent's king)

he is in check (Fig. 20). You don't have to do so but it's a good idea to say 'check' to warn your opponent that his king is under attack. If you are in check you must do something about it. In this position White must move his king to a safe square.

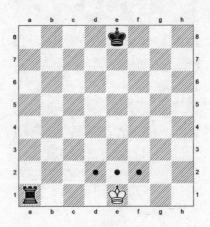

Fig. 20

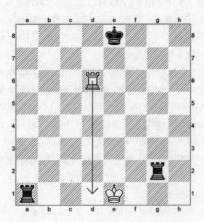

Fig. 21

In Fig. 21 White has no safe squares for his king. He can get out of check, though, by moving his rook to d1 to block the black rook's attack on his king.

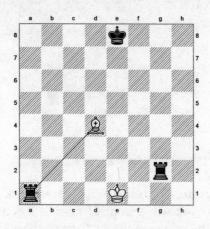

Fig. 22

In Fig. 22 White can (and must) get out of check by capturing the black rook with his bishop. It's also possible to get out of check by making a capture with your king, either of the checking piece or of another piece, as long as your king ends up on a square in which he's safe from capture.

To sum up: if your opponent plays a move that attacks your king you are in check. If you are in check you have to do something about it. There are three potential ways of getting out of check: moving your king to a safe square, blocking the check (only available if you are in check from a rook, bishop or queen) and capturing the checking piece, either with your king or with another piece.

9. Checkmate

In Fig. 23 Black has just moved his rook to a1. White is in check and has no way out. He has no safe square for his king, cannot block the check and cannot capture the checking piece.

Fig. 23

This is checkmate. The game stops here. Black has won the game. The way you win a game of chess is by checkmate. You don't capture the king or remove it from the board, rather, if you like, you trap the king.

Fig. 24

Another checkmate position is shown in Fig. 24. Remember that two kings cannot stand next to each other, so White cannot capture the black queen. Again the game is over and Black has won.

10. Stalemate

Fig. 25

In Fig. 25 it's White's move. He is not in check at the moment. However he has no legal moves at all. Has he lost the game?

Not at all. If it's your move and you have no legal moves (moves which do not leave your king in check with any of your pieces) it's stalemate. The result of the game is a draw. If White had a pawn on, say, a3, it wouldn't be stalemate as he would be able to move his pawn.

Note that if it was Black's move here he could get checkmate by moving his queen to e2.

Some people think that 'stalemate' just means that your king cannot move. Not true at all. If it were true, the starting position would be stalemate!

11. Other Draws

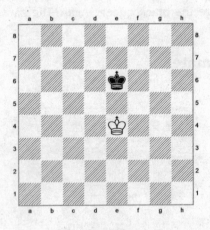

Fig. 26

If you reach a position from which it is impossible for either side to deliver checkmate the game is an automatic draw. King against king, as in Fig. 26, is an obvious example. King and bishop against king and king and knight against king are also drawn for the same reason. (Try it out for yourself if you don't believe me.)

There are other types of draw which you don't need to know at this point, but your children will need to know them if they want to take part in competitions. They will be dealt with in a later chapter of the book.

12. Castling

There's just one more rule to learn, and it's an important one which many players get wrong. Castling is a special move which involves moving the king two squares towards the rook and, in the same move, the rook jumping over the king to the next square.

Fig. 27

In Fig. 27 (assuming the kings and rooks haven't moved) either player may castle on either side of the board.

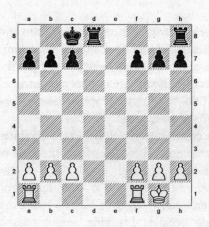

Fig. 28

In Fig. 28 White has castled on the king side (the side where the king started: e-h files) and Black has castled on the queen side (the side where the queen started: a-d files). Note that the white king is nearer the corner while the black king is nearer the centre.

Fig. 29

There are several restrictions on when you can castle:

You cannot castle if you have moved your king or your rook (even if you have moved them back to their starting square).

You cannot castle if you are in check (contrary to what many people think it doesn't matter if you've been in check as long as you haven't moved your king).

You cannot castle into check (in Fig. 29 White cannot castle because he would end up in check from the rook on g8).

You cannot castle through check. This is the hard one to understand: you cannot castle if your king crosses a square controlled by an enemy piece. In Fig. 29 Black cannot castle on the queen side because his king would cross d8, which is controlled by the white rook on d1.

21

WINNING AT CHESS

So you've learnt (or reminded yourself of) the moves. Now you need to teach your children.

They'll need to play regularly (once a week at school is not enough) in order to get a feel for the game. If you don't play at all against them they'll make little progress, but if you play badly against them they'll develop bad habits which they'll find hard to get rid of. They'll also lose regularly at their school chess club to children who have been taught by their parents to play well. I see so many children in school chess clubs who start the game with the worst possible moves – because they're the moves their parents play against them.

You don't have to be a good player to play your children, but you have to know enough to recognise good play when you see it.

Parents often tell me how much their young children enjoy playing chess when they are doing no more than playing random moves. You're only really playing chess if you understand the logic of chess and have a basic appreciation of simple tactics and strategy. If you don't have these skills yourself, you'll need to acquire them, and, believe me, you'll find it very much easier to learn this than your children will.

The underlying logic
The underlying logic of the game can be reduced to three words: Superior Force Wins (SFW).

For the benefit of less experienced players we assign values to the different pieces:

- Pawn: 1 point
- Knight: 3 points
- Bishop: 3 points
- Rook: 5 points
- Queen: 9 points

(These are not particularly accurate and tend to undervalue the queen – 10 may be nearer the mark and, to a lesser extent, the bishop, especially when one player has two bishops against bishop and knight or two knights, but they are good enough for beginners. In any case they are only averages: there are positions where, for example, a knight is better than a rook.)

In brief, other things being equal, in a game between two equally matched experienced players, a player with two extra points would, in most cases, expect to win fairly easily, and a player with one extra point would expect to win more often than not.

So our first aim is to ensure that we have a bigger and stronger army than our opponent. To do this we must do three things:

1. Check whether we can make a move which wins material (points) either by capturing an enemy piece for nothing, or by trading a weaker piece (or combination of pieces) for a stronger piece (or combination of pieces). Thus we should normally, for instance, be happy to trade off one of our bishops for an enemy rook.
2. Notice whether our opponent is trying to win material (by taking one of our pieces for free or by trading one of his weaker pieces for one of our stronger pieces). If he has a threat we must meet it by: (a) moving it to safety, (b) defending it with another piece, (c) capturing the attacker, (d) blocking the threat by interposing another piece or (e) creating an equal or bigger threat (EBT) somewhere else.
3. (And this is by far the hardest) Make sure that the move we are making is not going to allow our opponent to win points.

Mistakes can be made in this way by (a) moving a piece to a square where it can be captured safely, (b) moving away a piece which was defending an enemy target, (c) closing a line of defence or (d) moving a pinned piece (opening a line of attack).

Our first aim when learning chess is to develop our chessboard vision and self-discipline so that we never (or at least hardly ever) make one-move oversights of this nature.

If we have more pawns than our opponent we can use them to get some queens and checkmate him. If we have more pieces than our opponent we might use them to get checkmate if his king isn't safe. More often we'll identify targets (pawns that cannot be defended by their fellows) and attack them with more pieces than he can defend them. It's easier to do this if we trade off our opponent's more powerful pieces first.

If you think about it, an army of 1,000 men is not much stronger than an army of 999 men, but an army of two men is twice as strong as an army of one man. Logically, therefore, by the principle of proportion, if we're ahead we'll try to exchange our pieces for enemy pieces of equal value, and if we're behind we'll try to avoid exchanges. However, the more pawns you have the easier it is to promote one of them, so if we're ahead we're usually trying to exchange pieces but not pawns, and if we're behind we're usually trying to exchange pawns but not pieces.

So, if you want to beat your kids at chess, the first thing you have to do is avoid one-move oversights.

Tactics

Consider the game of noughts and crosses. We lose if we overlook our opponent's threat and we let him make a line. We lose when our opponent creates two threats at once. If we look far enough ahead we can see a potential double threat coming and always at least draw the game with best play.

Chess works in the same way but at a much higher level. We can sometimes win material by creating two threats at the same time, either with the same piece or with different pieces. With any luck our opponent won't be able to meet both threats. Sometimes we can even play a sacrifice: we can give up a bishop because we've seen that in two moves' time we can win a rook. We can even give up a queen because we've seen that in three moves' time we can get checkmate. We can also make use of non-simultaneous double threats: for instance by capturing or driving away a defending piece.

If we look ahead we can see these opportunities. We can also look ahead and try to prevent our opponent making moves like this.

How can we look ahead when both players may have 30 or 40 moves to choose from? Exactly: that's what makes chess so hard. We learn to look for forcing moves: checks, captures and threats, and calculate ahead as far and as accurately as we can. Easy for computers but hard for humans. It takes a lot of practice.

We can train ourselves by spending time every day solving puzzles. There are plenty of good puzzle books available and also several free websites which offer thousands of puzzles for us to solve.

In positions where there are no strong forcing moves available and where we don't have any threats to meet (which is most positions) we're thinking about strategy as well as tactics.

Strategy

Strategy involves putting pieces on good squares and forming plans. At this point we don't need to worry too much about long-range plans. Putting pieces on good squares, though, is essential. If we position our pieces effectively the tactics will work in our favour. If we position our pieces ineffectively the tactics will work against us. So we are trying to keep our pieces on effective squares and, at the same time, keep the enemy pieces away from effective squares.

Effective squares for the big guys at the back are squares that are both strong and safe. Strong squares are, by and large, squares which give pieces plenty of options and don't get in the way of other pieces. Queens, bishops and knights all control more squares in the centre of the board than from the sides or corners, so we're trying to occupy or control the squares in the centre. Line pieces (queen, rooks, bishops) can also be effective working together on the same line. A safe square is, by and large again, a square on which a piece will not be attacked and driven back to a less effective square.

Pawns need to be treated separately. We try to maintain a strong pawn formation. Weak pawns are pawns which are open to attack from enemy pieces and which cannot call upon a friendly pawn for support.

Finally, and most importantly, we need to keep our king safe from attack, behind a wall of pawns and with some pieces around to defend him. We usually do this by castling.

Openings

With a basic knowledge of strategy we can work out what we should be doing in the opening.

We start by putting a pawn in the centre of the board. We're going to use our e-pawn, d-pawn and often also our c-pawn to fight for control of the centre.

We're going to bring out (develop) our knights and bishops as quickly as we can, onto squares where they'll help us fight for the centre.

We're probably going to castle quickly, usually on the king side where it's safer, and we're going to keep the f-, g- and h-pawns at home to defend the king. Castling will also help us to connect our rooks in the centre of the board.

We're going to keep our queen somewhere in the centre where she's not exposed to attack. We probably won't be doing too much with her early on, but because she's such a strong piece we're always going to be looking out for tactical opportunities.

We're probably not going to do too much with the rooks early on either – and we're certainly not going to develop them via a3 and h3. Instead we're going to keep them on the back rank and move them to any files which might get opened up as a result of pawn exchanges.

Even though we're thinking about where we put our pieces at the start of the game we're not going to forget about tactics. We're going to look for every check, capture and threat, both for us and for our opponent, we're going to make sure we don't play moves that lose material without a very good reason, and we're going to check every move to see if we can play a move that wins material.

Putting it Together

Now we've got some idea of what we're trying to do during a game of chess let's play a few moves together and see what happens.

In this section we'll be using chess notation. If we move a pawn we'll just refer to the square the pawn moves to: so 'e4' means the pawn moves to e4. If we move a piece we'll prefix this with the initial letter of the piece (using N for knight and K for king), for instance Nf3. Note the upper case letter for the piece and the lower case letter for the square.

Fig. 30

Just to remind you, Fig. 30 shows the starting position. At present there are no moves that will win the game for you, and also none that will lose the game. Some moves are better than others, though.

We're going to play in the centre, remember, and we need to make space for our pieces, so we'll start by moving one of our centre pawns two squares. We'll play the move e4. As it happens, d4 is equally popular and strong, but e4 is easier to understand so it's the move we usually teach beginners. By playing this move we're opening up lines for our bishop and queen, and therefore moving one step towards castling should the need arise.

We'll give Black the same move for the same reasons: e5. Other moves are also popular and good but again this is the easiest move to understand. (Fig. 31.)

Fig. 31

Now White should start thinking about developing his minor pieces (knights and bishops). The most popular move here is Nf3 so that's what we'll play. Knights prefer to be in the centre of the board, and by developing his king-side pieces White is again one step closer to being able to castle. There's another reason for choosing this move as well.

Black now stops to look at White's move. Is there a threat? Yes, there is. White is threatening to capture the pawn on e5. Black certainly shouldn't even consider any move that gives up this pawn for nothing. The pawn can't move so we're going to have to defend it. (Actually, counter-attacking with Nf6 is also possible as long as you know what you're doing.) There are several ways in which Black can do this. We're not going to play f6 because it weakens our king side defences and takes away a good square from the knight on g8. We're not going to play Bd6: it's an ineffective square for the bishop and blocks in the d-pawn which we want to move to develop the bishop on c8. We're not going to play Qe7 (blocking the bishop on f8) or Qf6 (taking f6 away from the knight on g8) because we don't want to bring our queen out too soon to a square where she might be attacked, for example, by a knight on d5. We could play d6, even though it blocks in the bishop on f8, but the usual move is to play Nc6.

Note how we're listing the moves which are tactically viable and comparing them on strategic grounds.

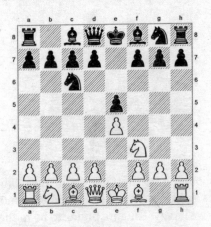

Fig. 32

We now have a typical situation: attacker (N on f3), target (P on e5), defender (N on c6). Black has no threats so White has a free hand in what he plays next. (Fig. 32.)

There are four sensible moves here which help us develop and control the centre. Simplest, perhaps, is to bring out our other knight to c3. We can also develop our bishop on f1. Bb5, attacking the knight that's defending the pawn, is a very strong move which has always been popular at the top level of chess. Bc4 is also very popular, particularly with young children, and rightly so because it targets the f7 square which is the weak point in Black's position. But we're going to choose another excellent move for White: d4. Before playing this we have to see that Black could take it in two ways and make sure the move is not losing material. We check it out: Black could play exd4 (note 'x' indicates a capture, and we specify the file for a pawn capture: it's usually best to capture with the lower valued piece if your opponent can take back, and often best to capture with the higher valued piece if he can't take back) and White could play Nxd4. Black could then play Nxd4 and we're in luck: White would reply with Qxd4.

Fig. 33

After d4 Black again has to meet a threat. (This is typical: White has a nominal advantage at the start of the game because he can attack while Black has to defend.) This time Black chooses to capture with exd4, which is undoubtedly his best move. (Fig. 33.)

Now White's obvious move is to recapture with the knight (certainly not with the queen): Nxd4, so that's what we'll play.

Black has to consider whether or not to take the white knight. In fact it's not the best move. (After Nxd4 Qxd4 White's queen is strongly placed in the centre. Black could threaten her with c5 but that would leave him with a weakened pawn formation: his d-pawn would become a target for White's pieces as it could no longer call on the c-pawn for support.) White now has a slight advantage in the centre but, to compensate, Black is now able to start creating his own threats while developing his king-side pieces and preparing to castle. Bc5, to attack the knight again, is a good move, and so is Nf6, to threaten the pawn on e4. That's the move we'll play here. (Fig. 34.)

Note that once there's been a pawn exchange in the centre both players will hurry to get their king to safety behind a wall of pawns by castling.

Fig. 34

Now it's White's turn to meet a threat. He can't afford to lose his e4 pawn for nothing. He could advance it to e5 but a quick check reveals that it's not safe: the knight on c6 could capture it. So he needs to use another piece to defend his pawn.

This position shows you how easy it is to make one-move blunders. It's natural to play Bd3 to defend the e-pawn and prepare to castle, but that would be a bad mistake. It closes the queen's line of defence and allows Black to capture the knight on d4 for free. An extra knight would give Black a winning advantage. It would be equally bad to play Qe2 or Qf3, making the error of moving a defender and again leaving the knight on d4 to be taken for free. So what else could White choose? Qd3 would expose the queen to a future attack and also blocks in the bishop on f1, while f3 would weaken the white king's defences. The obvious move then is to play Nc3, although Nxc6 is also popular.

White has created no threat so Black has a free choice. He wants to develop his bishop on f8 and castle to bring his king to safety. Bc5, attacking the knight on d4 again, would be a reasonable move. Instead we'll create a different threat by playing Bb4. (Fig. 35.)

Fig. 35

Again we stop and consider our opponent's last move carefully. Black is attacking the knight on c3, which is defended by the pawn on b2. But look again and you'll see also that the knight cannot move because it would leave the white king in check. This is a pin. So as well as attacker b4, target c3, defender b2, we have attacker f6, target e4, defender – no defender because the knight on c3 is pinned. We also have to remember attacker c6, target d4, defender d1. Yes, chess is complicated! White has to meet the threat to his pawn on e4. Bd3 again is no good as it blocks the queen's defence of d4. Qe2 or Qf3 are again no good as they move the queen away from defending d4. Again, any of these moves will just lose the knight on d4 for nothing. Qd3 and f3 are still possible but open to the same objections as before. So White's best option is to capture the knight on c6: Nxc6.

Note that it's very often good to do what Black did here and position a line piece in line with a more valuable enemy piece. So can we line up our bishops on the same diagonal as an enemy rook, queen or king, our rooks on the same file as an enemy queen or king, and our queen on the same line as the enemy king?

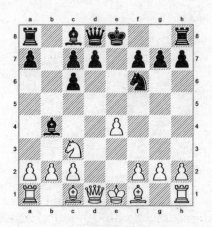

Fig. 36

Now Black has to recapture on c6 and must consider which of the two methods he prefers. Playing dxc6 would open up the d-file and allow White to trade queens and stop Black castling. So instead Black prefers to play bxc6. (Fig. 36.)

Now it's important that White doesn't forget about the threat to his e-pawn. It's a very easy mistake to make: only to look at the last move rather than the whole board, and to forget about what else is happening in the position. The chessboard's a big place and there can be a lot going on in different parts of the board.

White now has a convenient defence to his e-pawn: Bd3, developing a piece and preparing to castle.

White still has the advantage in the centre, but the exchange on c6 has given Black an extra pawn in that zone, so he decides to use it to challenge White's central superiority and play d5. (Fig. 37.)

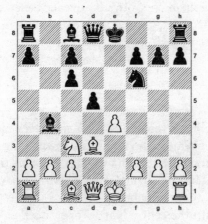

Fig. 37

Yet again White has to meet a threat to his e-pawn. He has two reasonable choices: to trade pawns on d5 or to advance to e5, threatening the black knight on f6. Advancing a pawn to threaten a knight is often good, but here White judges that after Ng4 his e-pawn will be somewhat exposed so he decides to trade pawns instead by playing exd5.

Black can take back in three ways but it's obvious and best to take back with the pawn. Why? Because it gives him a pawn in the centre and because he doesn't like having two pawns on the same file. (Two pawns on the same file – doubled pawns – are often, but not always, a liability.) (Fig. 38.)

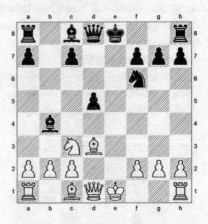

Fig. 38

Finally, White has a respite. Black is no longer making threats, but it is he, not White, who now has a pawn in the middle. Black has some central advantage now but at the same time his d- and c-pawns might be open to attack while White's pawns are safe at home. Swings and roundabouts.

Anyway, with the centre blasted open it's high time for both players to get their kings into safety before something nasty happens on the e-file.

So White castles (we write o-o for king-side castling and o-o-o for queen-side castling) and Black follows suit. (Fig. 39.)

Hereabouts Black has the choice of trading bishop for knight on c3, giving White doubled c-pawns.

One of the most interesting things about chess – perhaps THE most interesting thing – is that we have two pieces of very similar strength but very different powers. Bishops, fast-moving line pieces but confined to squares of one colour, prefer open positions such as this. Knights, slow-moving jumpers, prefer closed positions where they can jump in and out while the bishops are stuck behind pawns.

If Black makes the trade he will weaken White's pawn formation but give him the better minor pieces in exchange. Swings and roundabouts again.

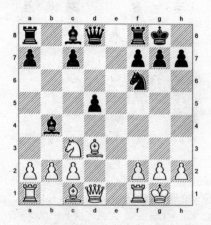

Fig. 39

Now White has the chance to create a threat. He wants to develop his last minor piece so his natural move is Bg5, pinning the knight on f6.

This is a positional (strategic) threat rather than a threat to win material. White wants to play Bxf6. If Black then recaptures with the Queen, his d-pawn will no longer be defended and White will be able to play Nxd5. If instead he recaptures with the g-pawn he will have doubled pawns in front of his king, leaving His Majesty open to attack.

Black can meet this threat by defending his d-pawn again so that he'll be able to capture with the queen should White take on f6. Be6 would be a natural developing move but would tie that piece down to defence when it might have a brighter future elsewhere. So instead Black chooses c6, preferring to use a pawn rather than a bishop as a defender. (Fig. 40.)

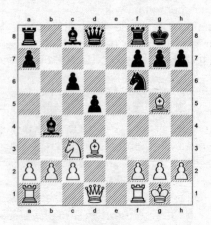

Fig. 40

We'll leave the game here and just add that the position offers equal chances.

Those moves should give you some idea about what good chess is about and about the thought processes your children need to develop (and you need to develop in order to help them).

Yes, chess is complicated, and this was a relatively simple example. There are many other openings that are much more complicated, strategically, tactically or both.

In fact, these moves are all well known (a commercially available database includes more than 4,000 games reaching this position) and any serious player who includes this variation in his opening repertoire will know them off by heart, but it's a good idea to go through the thought processes again every time you play them.

PART TWO

A CHESS COURSE FOR JUNIOR SCHOOL AGE CHILDREN

This course is based on the chessKIDS academy website and my book *Chess for Kids*.

It is suitable for children of age 7 upwards. Some younger children (age 5 or 6) may be able to access it as well, but be prepared to hold back if they find anything too hard. I am also working on a very different approach to learning chess which will be more suitable for older children (age 9 or 10 upwards).

The course teaches chess step by step, introducing each piece in turn and giving children the chance to play mini-games which will both familiarise learners with the pieces and teach them thinking skills which can be applied both to chess and to other aspects of their lives.

The course is based on a series of online interactive lessons reinforced by quizzes. Children who answer all the quiz questions correctly receive a certificate. There are also videos covering each of the topics in the course. There are computer programs which will play the mini-games against you, as well as complete games once all the pieces have been learnt.

There is a facility to print out the moves of the student's games against the computer. You can then play through the games and discuss the moves together.

Another feature is the inclusion of tactics puzzles, some of which incorporate a worksheet generator which will produce random puzzle sheets for solving offline.

As this is a multi-media course you can choose which aspects of the course you use depending on your children's preferred learning style. For younger children, it's best if you familiarise yourself with the material first and then demonstrate the lesson to your children on an individual basis to ensure they've understood it. Children within the upper range of this age group may be able to teach themselves through the online interactive lessons.

The course exists online in two versions. The original version, which contains a lot of subversive humour, can be found at www.chesskids.me.uk. The 'straight' version is at www. chesskids.org.uk.

A hard copy version of the course, including worksheets, is available for free download from either of the above sites under the name 'Journey through Chess'.

1

THE BOARD AND PIECES

The first part of the course introduces the student to the chessboard and the pieces. Children learn to name the squares on the board and identify the pieces. They should also learn about the correct orientation of the board: white (light) on the right. Reinforce this every time you play. Try setting up the board the wrong way round occasionally and ask them if they see anything wrong. It's also worth introducing the concept of ranks (horizontal), files (vertical) and diagonals at this point and getting children to name the ranks and files. Naming the ranks can be confusing to children: if you're White, your second rank is numbered 2 but if you're Black, your second rank is numbered 7.

It's possible to skip this if you want your pupils to be able to play competitive games at once. It is useful, though, for children to learn the names of the squares for several reasons. You will need to make sure you're using a board with coordinates marked round the edges. If necessary you can write the letters and numbers on sticky paper and stick them to the board. This will also help with orientation of the board. Remember, also, that the white pieces start on the ranks numbered 1 and 2, and the black pieces on 7 and 8.

It's easier to refer to squares by name when teaching rather than saying 'that square over there'. Children who want to take the game seriously will need to write their moves down: this is much easier to learn if you have a fluent knowledge of the names of the squares. There are worksheets available on the site for this purpose along with interactive games where you have to either name or locate a particular square, either with or without coordinates.

Your children may want to learn about the pieces in the first lesson, but you might prefer not to teach this: it will be some time before they play a complete game and they are more likely to become impatient if they know too much about all the pieces. Make sure you teach children the correct names – it's a rook, remember, not a castle!

2

THE PAWN

In this chapter we're learning the pawn move and playing games with pawns.

Many courses start with the rook and bishop, which are easier to learn (the pawn has several different moves) but in some ways harder to handle because they have more possible moves.

Very young children will be better off starting with these pieces, or learning simpler strategy games before moving on to chess. However, most 7-year-olds and many younger children will have no problem picking up the pawn move especially as we're going to teach everything about the pawn one step at a time.

Start by explaining that the pawn can move one square forward. On its first move it has the choice of moving one or two squares forward.

Now we introduce the first Capture the Flag game. We ask the students to imagine that there's a flag at either end of the board. The first player to get a pawn to the other side captures the flag and wins the game. Explain that in chess, and also in the Capture the Flag games, White plays the first move, after which the players take it in turns to move.

Set up the position shown in Fig. 41 and give them the choice of White or Black. Ask the reason for their choice. At this point they will probably give an 'illogical' answer such as 'White, because it's my favourite colour' or 'Black, because then I can see what you do and copy your move'. Persuade them, if they need persuading, to play White. Ask who they think will win. They

Fig. 41

may well say something like 'You, because you're more experienced than me', which would be a good answer for a more complicated game, but not for this simple game. Ask (or remind) them about the pawn move and explain that they have a choice: to move one square or two squares forward. If necessary, continue questioning and asking until they tell you that they're going to move two squares forward, and that they will win by getting to the end first. Demonstrate this by getting them to play White against you. They'll probably be delighted to win. Now ask what would happen if White moved one square first. Turn the board round and ask them to play Black. Would they move one or two squares? Eventually they'll get the idea and see that if White moves one square they'll win by moving two squares but lose by moving one square.

This is an exercise in decision making skills. First of all, they will understand that chess is a game of skill, not a game of luck. It's about making decisions and in a full game of chess the player who makes the better decisions will win. They're learning the two stages of decision making: identifying their choices and looking ahead in order to make their choice.

Now set up a position with the pawns on different files (but at least two files apart) and ask your children whether they'd rather play White or Black. Continue this until they realise that the same principle applies each time: White will win if he chooses to advance his pawn two squares.

This exercise teaches analogical reasoning: they are learning to draw inferences from analogous positions and therefore make the correct move. Feel free to stop at this point, or at any time your children are beginning to lose interest or concentration. For most children, little and often will be the best approach.

Now we explain the next Capture the Flag rule. If you cannot make a move you lose the game. (Some teachers play this as a draw and some as a win for the player with more pawns: you can choose either of these options if you wish, but the computer on our website counts it as a loss. In 'big chess', if you are not in check and cannot make a move it's a draw.) Demonstrate a position with pawns on, for example, e4 (White) and e5 (Black) and explain that neither pawn can move – they are both stuck.

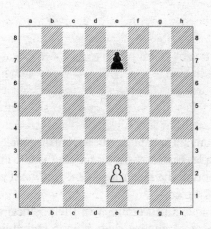

Fig. 42

Ask them to choose White or Black in the position shown in Fig. 42. If possible let them play Black but give them White if they insist. If you're playing White move your pawn two squares and explain that they have a choice. Will they move one or two squares? Repeat the rule that if you can't move you lose. Once they understand that if White moves two squares, Black will win at once by doing the same, start again, this time moving one square. Again, they have a choice. If they look ahead they'll see that they will win next move by moving one square, but lose next move by moving two squares. Can they find and verbalise the general rule in this position? Black can win by copying White's move.

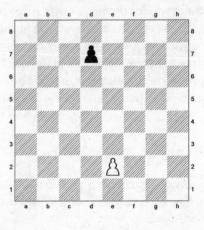

Fig. 43

Now explain that pawns capture one square diagonally forwards. Set up some examples to demonstrate and ask them to do the same.

Another Capture the Flag rule is that you win if you capture all your opponent's pieces.

Repeat the above procedure with the position shown in Fig. 43, asking them to choose their colour and their first move. Again, can they find the general rule? In this position Black will win as long as he does the opposite to White (if White moves one square Black must move two squares and vice versa).

Set up analogous positions of all three types: ask who will win and what the correct strategy is in each case. Ensure that they are using a combination of memory and analogical reasoning to reach the right answer every time.

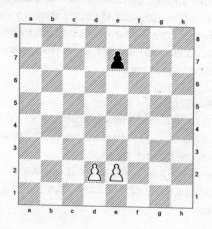

Fig. 44

Now ask who will win the position shown in Fig. 44 and why. You may well receive the correct answer: that White will win because he starts with more pawns.

Play it out – you will see that White will always win unless he makes a bad mistake.

This is our first introduction to the basic principle which underpins this course: SFW ((other things being equal) Superior Force (usually) Wins).

You can play these positions out against the computer if you want.

What happens when the computer loses? Is he a good sport or a bad loser? What happens when he wins? The computer's remarks in the humorous version of the course usually make children laugh. Use this, as and when appropriate, to discuss good sportsmanship. How should you react when you lose? What should you say to your opponent? What about when you win? You might like to encourage tournament etiquette: shake hands before and after the game, say 'good luck' before the game and 'well played' or 'good game' afterwards.

You might like to try positions with two pawns each. Try e2, d2 v e7, d7. An interesting one is e2, d2 v d7, c7. What happens with three pawns each? Invite your children to invent games of their own with pawns starting on different squares (but always with the correct pawn move).

At this point you might want to introduce the 'en passant' rule if you think your children will be able to understand it. Some children pick it up straight away but others go for years without really getting it at all. Your children will need to know it if they start playing competitively so you might think it a good idea to go through it quickly now and repeat it quickly every day. If you play the full pawn game against the computer you'll have plenty of chances to use it.

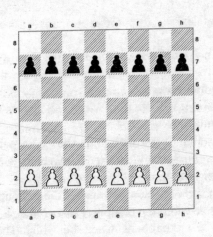

Fig. 45

Fig. 45 is the complete pawn game. You might like to start by letting your children play 8 pawns against 6 or 8 pawns against 7. When they can beat you at each level, move up to the higher level until you reach 8 pawns each. You can also play these games against the computer.

The first thing to look out for is to make sure they understand not to move a pawn to a square where it can be captured for free (unless you've looked ahead and have seen that you can get a pawn to the end first). This means paying attention, concentrating, watching your opponent's move and looking at the whole board all the time.

Because of this, children are often nervous about playing a move which allows their opponent to exchange pawns. They don't want to lose one of their pawns even if they get an enemy pawn in return. Other things being equal, exchanges are fine. Encourage them to look for opportunities to offer an exchange of pawns. On the other hand, if they have a chance to exchange they will usually avail themselves of the opportunity, in the hope that their opponent won't recapture – if you like a 'theory of mind' issue. It's sometimes a very hard lesson for children to learn that your opponents will try to play the best move, not what you want them to play.

Assuming no unforced errors, there are basically two ways of winning.

Usually you will win by running your opponent out of useful moves and forcing him to give up his pawns. You will usually have to be careful to make sure you have more 'spare moves' than your opponent. Very often you will reach a position towards the end of the game where you have a choice between advancing and exchanging a threatened pawn. Children will usually choose to exchange for the reason given above, but often it's better to advance so that your opponent has to use up one of his spare pawn moves.

In this game White has to make the critical decision on move 11. Play the game through together and decide what you would do at that point. You should be able to work out that if White moves to e4, as he did in the game, he will win, but if he takes on f4 instead he will lose assuming Black recaptures.

1. d2-d3 e7-e5 2. c2-c4 g7-g5 3. b2-b3 f7-f5 4. e2-e3 c7-c5 5. g2-g3 h7-h5 6. f2-f3 a7-a5 7. h2-h4 g5xh4 8. g3xh4 d7-d6 9. a2-a3 b7-b6 10. a3-a4 f5-f4 (Fig. 46.)

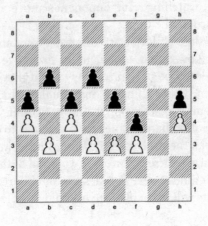

Fig. 46

11. e3-e4 d6-d5 12. c4xd5 b6-b5 13. d5-d6 b5xa4 14. d6-d7 a4xb3 15. d7-d8

The other way to win is to create a Passed Pawn. A passed pawn is a pawn which can reach the end of the board without being blocked or captured by an enemy pawn. Creating a passed pawn before your opponent and pushing it to the end of the board as quickly as you can will win you the game. This is an important idea in king and pawn endings in 'big chess' as well, so this knowledge may well come in very useful in a year or two's time.

Play through the following game (or better still get your pupil to play through it to practise reading chess notation) and see how White wins by creating a passed pawn.

1. c2-c3 e7-e5 2. d2-d4 e5xd4 3. c3xd4 d7-d5 4. f2-f3 a7-a5
5. e2-e4 d5xe4 6. f3xe4 g7-g5 7. e4-e5 h7-h5 8. d4-d5 b7-b5
(Fig. 47.)

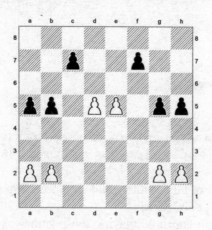

Fig. 47

9. e5-e6 f7xe6 10. d5xe6 c7-c5 11. e6-e7 h5-h4 12. e7-e8

Finally, children enjoy seeing – and playing – games like the following where Black wins by copying White until the point where White has to give away his pawns.

1. f2-f4 f7-f5 2. d2-d4 d7-d5 3. b2-b4 b7-b5 4. h2-h4 h7-h5
5. g2-g3 g7-g6 6. e2-e3 e7-e6 7. c2-c3 c7-c6 8. a2-a3 a7-a6 (Fig. 48.)

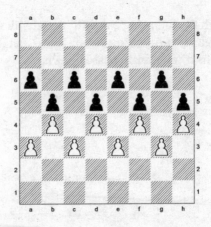

Fig. 48

9. g3-g4 h5xg4 10. h4-h5 g6xh5 11. e3-e4 d5xe4 12. d4-d5 e6xd5
13. c3-c4 b5xc4 14. a3-a4 c4-c3 15. b4-b5 c6xb5 16. a4xb5 a6xb5

Can you think of how White could stop this happening? Do you
think Black will always win?

Children can continue playing these games as long as they
like. Ideally, they shouldn't move on until they can play the
complete pawn game without making avoidable one-move
oversights, and have started to acquire the skill of being able to
choose between moves by looking ahead to what's going to
happen next.

3
THE ROOK

The rook move is easy to understand for most children, although some younger children lack the hand-eye-brain coordination to be able to follow a straight line from one end of the board to the other.

In this chapter we also introduce the vital concepts of threats, attack and defence.

It's a good idea to be very specific in the way you use the words 'threat' and 'attack'. If you don't do this it's very easy to cause confusion. I recommend using 'threat' to describe something you *want* to do next move and 'attack' to describe something you *could* do next move.

For some of the activities both here and later a supply of counters of different colours would be useful.

We now know two very different pieces. When you introduce the rook move, ask which piece is better, the rook or the pawn.

Set up some positions and ask your children to demonstrate the rook move by placing counters on the board to indicate where the rook can move (not forgetting to include captures). Add some enemy pawns and perhaps a rook. Ask your children to place counters on the board to indicate which of the rook's possible squares are safe. Explain the idea of safety if necessary: a safe square (for this purpose) is one where the rook will not be exposed to capture. Perhaps they could use green counters to indicate safe squares and red counters to indicate unsafe squares.

Because the rook is (other things being equal) stronger than the pawn, if we move a pawn to attack an enemy rook it's a threat. We'd love nothing better than to trade one of our pawns for an enemy rook. If we move a rook to attack an enemy pawn, it's only a threat if the pawn is not defended. We also need to be very sure we don't move our rook to a square where it can be taken by an enemy pawn.

Check that this concept is understood by setting up positions on the board and asking questions. How can your pawn threaten my rook? How can your rook attack my pawn? Is it an attack or a threat?

Demonstrate a position where a rook threatens our pawn but we can defend by moving a rook so that if the rook captures we can take back. Demonstrate a position where a rook threatens a pawn but we can move another pawn to defend it. Ask your children some questions on this theme. Which pawn is being threatened? How can you use a rook to defend the pawn? Ensure that the concepts of attack and defence are fully understood before moving on. Ask your children to make up some quiz questions themselves.

Another way to look at it which might appeal to boys is this. In a real fight little guys run away from big guys but big guys stay put and defend themselves when attacked by little guys. But because you take it in turns in chess the opposite is true. If a pawn attacks a rook, the rook must run away. But if a rook attacks a pawn, the pawn is happy to stay there as long as he has someone to protect him. He doesn't mind losing his life as long as his army takes an enemy life in exchange.

Once your children have understood this concept you can move onto the first rook game. At this point we have to make a slight change to our 'Capture the Flag' rules. From now on, to win the game, if you get a pawn to the end it becomes a queen (pawn promotion): to win the game you have to play a move with the queen. In other words if your opponent gets a pawn to the end, you have one move in which to capture it if you can. You might want to add a very quick explanation of the queen move.

At this stage you could also briefly introduce the concept of the double threat. Demonstrate this by placing, for instance, black pawns on b7 and f7 and a white rook on d1. Now the rook can move to d7 to threaten both pawns. Whichever pawn moves away, you'll be able to take the other one. Creating two threats in different directions like this is called a fork. You can also do the same thing but in the same direction: move the pawn from f7 to a7, for instance. Now moving the rook to d7 creates only one direct threat, to b7, but if that pawn moves, White will be able to capture on a7 safely. We might say that there's an indirect threat to a7 and consider that, although not a fork, this is still a sort of double attack.

Now we can play a Capture the Flag game with a rook against some pawns. If your children are not confident, start with, say, a white rook on h1 against a black pawn on c7. Ask how White can win at once. Some children are tempted to threaten the pawn by moving to h7, but this allows the pawn to move up the board. Children will be able to work out that they can win at once by moving to their rook to c1. If you're trying to stop just one pawn you do so vertically, by occupying the enemy pawn's file with your rook. Now add another pawn, if you like on d7. Now if White moves to c1, the pawn can move to c6 where it's defended by the pawn on d7. It's still easy to win this way, but the easiest way is to move to h7 on your first move. Now, if the d-pawn moves you can capture the c-pawn instead.

When you're ready, the main version of the first game is rook against five pawns: something like Fig. 49.

With best play the rook should win. It needs a bit of care and forethought, though. The first danger is that White, just as Sam does in *Chess for Kids*, rushes to take as many pawns as he can without stopping to think about whether or not he can get back in time to stop an advancing pawn. The second danger is that White plays too defensively, trying to stop the enemy pawns too soon and not capturing enough pawns himself.

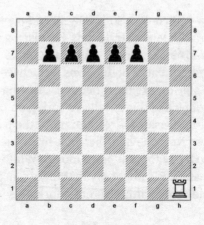

Fig. 49

Of course, White must also be careful not to place his rook where it can be captured by a black pawn. The mistake that most children make over and over again is to play a move impulsively without checking first to 'see' whether or not it's safe. It's a question of disciplining yourself to stop and ask yourself 'is it safe?' before playing every move in every game. Once you get used to it, this only takes a second or two. Many children, however, lack the self-discipline to do this.

It's worth playing this position out with both colours. If you wish you could add another pawn or two if your children are playing Black against you. Playing the pawns teaches you how pawns can work together.

Once this has been mastered you can move onto the complete rook game, as shown in Fig. 50.

For children who lack confidence: start with just one rook and eight pawns against eight pawns. This should pose no problems. Then move onto two rooks and eight pawns against one rook and eight pawns. This can be hard for some children.

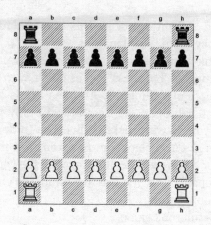

Fig. 50

Sometimes they will find it hard to make progress because they do not understand how to open up the position for their extra rook. If this is the case, explain that they need to open up lines for their rooks. They can do this by making pawn breaks (sometimes called pawn levers). Demonstrate by moving pawns to, for example, e4 and e5. Now explain that White might want to play d4 but at the moment it wouldn't be safe. He can prepare the move by playing another piece where it controls d4. This could be done by moving the pawn on c2 to c3 or by moving a rook to d1. Then, when White plays d4, if Black takes, White will be able to take back, and otherwise White will take on e5 himself.

Another useful technique is the team attack. This involves attacking a target with more than one piece, in this case two rooks. Any pawn that cannot be defended by another pawn is a potential target. Select your target and threaten it with a rook. Your opponent will probably move a rook to defend it. Now attack it with the other rook as well, and, with two attackers against one defender you'll be able to take it safely.

Many children are afraid to use either of these techniques because they don't want to lose one of their pieces even if they're going to make a profit out of it. This is a fundamental logical error which may require explanation.

The full rook game will teach you some lessons about using rooks which apply to 'big chess' just as much as to this game.

First, a couple of definitions. An open file is a file with no pawns on it. A half-open file is a file with only pawns of one colour. What you do with rooks is this. You trade some pawns, using pawn breaks. You place your rooks on open files or on your half-open files. If you're controlling an open file you can use it as a highway to enable your rooks to penetrate the enemy position and capture some pawns.

Look at this full rook game.

1. e2-e4 Ra8-d8 2. d2-d4 d7-d5 3. e4xd5 Rd8xd5 4. c2-c3 a7-a5
5. Rh1-e1 e7-e6 6. Ra1-d1 c7-c5 7. d4xc5 Rd5xc5 (Fig. 51.)

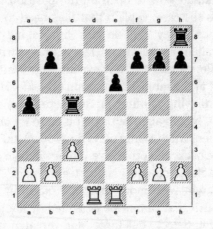

Fig. 51

8. Rd1-d7 b7-b5 9. Rd7xf7 e6-e5 10. Rf7xg7 h7-h5 11. Rg7-e7
Rh8-f8 12. f2-f3 Rf8-f4 13. Re7xe5 Rc5xe5 14. Re1xe5 h5-h4
15. Re5-e4 Rf4-f5 16. Re4xh4 a5-a4 17. Rh4-b4 Rf5-h5 18. h2-

h3 Rh5-g5 19. g2-g4 Rg5-c5 20. h3-h4 a4-a3 21. b2xa3 Rc5xc3
22. Rb4xb5 Rc3xa3 23. h4-h5 Ra3xa2 24. h5-h6 Ra2-f2 25.
Rb5-h5 Rf2xf3 26. h6-h7 Rf3-g3 27. h7-h8Q Rg3xg4 28. Qh8-h7

The pawn exchange on move 7 leaves White with control of the
open d-file which he uses to invade the seventh rank and capture
some black pawns.

Children don't need to master this game before moving on,
but they should be able to win games with two rooks against one
prior to progressing to the next piece.

4

THE BISHOP

The bishop should be no problem for most children, although some younger children will find it difficult to follow diagonals and will need some practice just moving the pieces around.

The concepts are similar to the rook, so you might like to use the time when your children are learning the bishop to talk more about the decision making process: about how chess is a game of skill and the winner will be the player who makes the best decisions.

Demonstrate the bishop move just as you did the rook move. Ask the pupils to place counters on the board to indicate the squares to which the bishop can move. If you like, add some pawns, and, if you like, rooks, and get the pupils to indicate the safe and unsafe bishop moves.

Then, ask the students to use a bishop to stop a single pawn. Then, use a bishop to stop two pawns on adjacent files. This should be fairly easy, but there are other questions you might like to investigate. How far up the board do the two pawns start for them to beat a bishop? How far apart do two pawns have to start for them to beat a bishop? It's good to allow time for children to make these investigations and perhaps make up some of their own.

Three pawns on adjacent files against a bishop (as shown in Fig. 52) is a challenging game, and not so easy to play well. The pawns should win with best play but the strategy is counter-intuitive. It might seem natural, as it does to Sam in *Chess for*

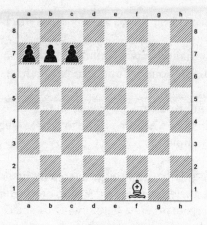

Fig. 52

Kids, to place your pawns on the opposite colour square to the enemy bishop so that they're immune from capture.

But watch what can happen.

1. Bf1-g2 b7-b5 2. Bg2-c6 b5-b4 3. Bc6-a4 c7-c5 4. Ba4-b3 a7-a5 5. Bb3-c4 a5-a4 6. Bc4-b5 a4-a3 7. Bb5-c4 (Fig. 53.)

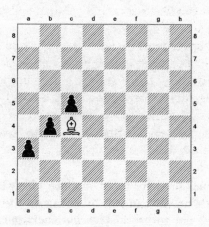

Fig. 53

7... a3-a2 8. Bc4xa2 b4-b3 9. Ba2xb3 c5-c4 10. Bb3xc4

Black sets up a chain of pawns but the white bishop occupies the a2-h7 diagonal and, one by one, the pawns have to fall on the sword.

Black can win by placing his pawns on the same colour square as the enemy bishop when he is able to do so safely.

Here's an example:

1. Bf1-g2 c7-c6 2. Bg2-e4 a7-a5 3. Be4-c2 b7-b5 4. Bc2-e4 c6-c5
5. Be4-c6 b5-b4 6. Bc6-d5 a5-a4 7. Bd5-c6 (Fig. 54.)

Fig. 54

7... b4-b3 8. Bc6xa4 c5-c4 9. Ba4-c6 c4-c3 10. Bc6-e4 c3-c2 and Black wins

Note that if Black saves his pawn on move 7 he will lose as in the first game. Instead, he can win by giving up the pawn as long as he's careful not to get his pawns blockaded by the white bishop.

This is a difficult game to play perfectly and children will be unlikely to master it at this stage in their development. It does, however, lead to interesting situations for discussion between teacher and pupil in terms of considering alternatives, looking ahead and making decisions.

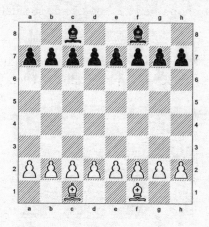

Fig. 55

Fig. 55 shows the complete bishop game. Just as with the rook, less confident children can start with one bishop and eight pawns against eight pawns, then two bishops and eight pawns against one bishop and eight pawns, or the teacher can play without a couple of pawns.

Ask your children which they think is more powerful and why: a rook or a bishop. If they are not sure about this (or even if they are) demonstrate by placing a rook and a bishop in turn on a central square and marking with counters the squares they control. They'll count 14 for a rook and 13 for a bishop. Now do the same using a corner square instead. This time a rook still controls 14 squares (which is why they start in the corner) but a bishop only controls seven squares. You could also explain (if they haven't already done so) that a bishop can only ever visit half the squares on the board.

You can also demonstrate by playing, for instance, two rooks and eight pawns against two bishops and eight pawns, with the student taking the rooks, or simply one rook and eight pawns against one bishop and eight pawns.

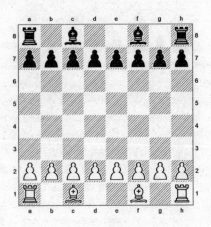

Fig. 56

You can also play the complete rook and bishop game (as shown in Fig. 56), to practise playing more complicated positions and learn how bishops and rooks can work together.

When your students are confident about using the bishop you can move on.

5

THE QUEEN

The queen move will be no problem for children who have mastered the rook and bishop moves. The problem comes with the number of choices you have available. The more choices you have the harder it becomes for you to consider all of them and make the correct decision. Because the queen is the most powerful piece on the board it's also (apart from the special case of the king) the most important: you have to be very careful not to lose it.

One of the lessons we reinforce at this point is that of checking that your move is safe before playing it. Set up some puzzles with queens on the board along with rooks and bishops and ask the pupils to mark safe squares for the queen with green counters and unsafe squares with red counters. Set up positions on the board where the queen can capture a pawn (which may or may not be defended) and ask if the capture is safe.

Fig. 57 is the basic queen against pawns game. Less confident children can start by playing against fewer pawns if they wish. Two things to note: we start with the pawn on d6 so that White can't take a pawn at once; and when you're playing the computer you'll find Black's pawn will promote into a rook which he has to move to win the game.

White should have few problems winning this game. The difficulties arise, just as with the rook, by panicking and trying to stop an enemy pawn before you need to do so rather than capturing as many pawns as you can before the opposing pawns get too far down the board.

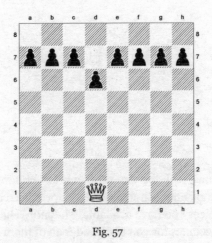

Fig. 57

If you find this too easy you can add another pawn on d7. If you don't have another set use a white pawn instead.

The trick is to use the double threat, or fork. In the starting position White has the choice of several moves which threaten two enemy pawns at the same time. Ask your children how many they can find. When you have a choice of captures, choose the one which will itself be a fork and will enable you to capture another pawn next move. Discuss the idea of forks as you play through the games: it will come in very useful in future. Set up positions where you have to find queen forks of, for example, an enemy bishop and rook. (To be safe, this will have to be on the same diagonal as the rook and the same rank or file as the bishop.)

Fig. 58 is the complete queen game. If you want, take off a couple of pawns to start with. This game can be trickier than most against the computer because the queen is so powerful. Ask which pawns could White move which would release the queen from the back rank. Perhaps it's best to start with one of these pawns. Another tip – and again an important concept for later on in your chess career – if you're ahead on pawns it may well be a good idea to try to exchange queens. Why do you think that is?

Fig. 58

Fig. 59

You can then move on and add rooks and/or bishops, perhaps reaching the position shown in Fig. 59. If you need to do so, play without some of your pieces against your children to give them a chance.

Another activity you can try with the queen is the Eight Queens Puzzle. You have to place eight queens on the board so that no two queens are attacking each other. In other words they must all be on a different rank, file and diagonal. If you don't have eight queens you can use pawns instead.

When your children are confident about harnessing the queen's power they can move onto the trickiest piece on the board, the knight.

6

THE KNIGHT

The knight is a hard piece to explain and understand. Start by placing a knight on a centre square and explain the move. Ask your students to place pawns or counters on the board to indicate the squares to which the knight can move. Ask them to describe what they see on the board. They may describe the shape or pattern, but they should also notice that all the squares are of the same colour: the opposite colour to the square where the knight is now.

You can describe the move to children as being in the shape of a letter L: two squares in a straight line followed by one round the corner but jumping over everything in its way. Some children might prefer a mathematical description. The knight moves to the opposite corner of a 3x2 rectangle. The knight moves to the nearest non-adjacent opposite coloured squares.

Practise the knight move by placing a white knight on a square and a black pawn on another square. Ask how many moves it takes the knight to reach the black pawn. How many different routes are there? Compare three squares away diagonally with two squares away diagonally: the knight can go from c3 to f6 in two moves but will take four moves to go from c3 to e5.

Start with the knight on a1. What is the quickest route to h8? You should be able to do it in 6 moves. Can you do it in 7 moves, or 8, or 9? Can they explain why? (As the knight moves to a different colour square each move it can only reach a square of the same colour in an even number of moves, and a square of the other colour in an odd number of moves.)

You could also try the knight tour. The knight has to visit every square of the board once only. Very hard, but not impossible. See how far you can get. Use counters to mark the squares already visited.

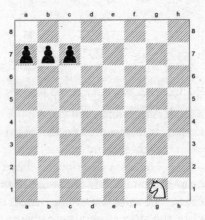

Fig. 60

It should be fairly easy for three pawns to beat the knight in the position shown in Fig. 60, but the knight should have no trouble dealing with two pawns on adjacent files. How far apart do two pawns have to be for them to defeat the knight?

Because knights, like queens, move in eight directions, they are particularly good at doing forks. At this point it's a good idea to practise some knight forks to get used to what they look like.

The knight game, as you might expect by now, looks like Fig. 61. As usual, children who are still struggling with the knight move can start with one knight and eight pawns against eight pawns, followed by two knights and eight pawns against one knight and eight pawns.

The big tip here is to look out for knight moves that fork two pawns. Remember that a fork involves two threats, not just two attacks. Keep on repeating the distinction between the two so

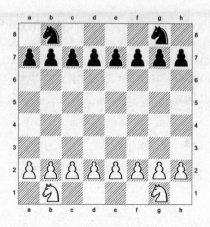

Fig. 61

that your students understand. Your opponent will have to move or defend one of them allowing you to win the other. Also try to look out for possible knight forks for your opponent. One way of preventing them is to advance a pawn to control the potential forking square.

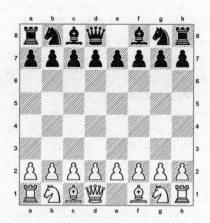

Fig. 62

You can also play games under Capture the Flag rules with all the pieces except the king, as in Fig. 62, or with any combination you choose. You can of course play with fewer pieces to make it fair, or, if by now your children are beating you, they could play with fewer pieces!

7
THE KING

The king has what appears to be the easiest move to understand, but in some ways it's just the opposite.

You can move any other piece to a square where it may be taken, but you are not allowed to move the king to a square where it may be taken. This difference between what you should not do and what you must not do is sometimes difficult for young children to grasp. With other pieces a move might be safe or unsafe. With the king it's legal or illegal.

One approach is to set up positions with a white king and various black pieces and ask the students to mark the adjacent squares to which the king could move legally with a counter. Don't forget they need to include captures as well as moves. To make sure they've considered every possibility they could mark legal moves with a green counter and illegal moves with a red counter.

Another activity you could try is a king maze, in which a king has to find the shortest route to reach a particular square.

You could also try a King Battle: start with the white king on e1 and the black king on e8. White has to try to get his king to the end of the board while Black has to try to stop him, or even get to the end first himself. Some of the concepts taught by this game will come in very useful later on when you get to study king and pawn endings.

At this point you're going to start playing to the full chess rules rather than the 'Capture the Flag' rules, although you might well want to go back and play some 'Capture the Flag' games at any point, either to reinforce a particular piece or as a quick activity at the end of a lesson.

You could, if you like, play a game of 'No Check Chess', with all the pieces but, unlike 'big chess' you can capture the king and win the game, but you might also think this will lead to confusion later on and prefer to move straight on to the next lesson.

8

CHECK, CHECKMATE AND STALEMATE

We're now coming to the most important part of the course. If you want to play a proper game of chess you really need to understand these concepts.

If you like you can use the examples in the Rules of Chess, Part One as a template.

Place the white king on, say, e1 and a black rook on a8. You might want to put a black king on e8 as well to make the position legal. Move the rook to a1. Explain that, because kings cannot be captured, if your king is attacked you have to do something about it. If you play a move which attacks the enemy king this is called a check. If you check your opponent's king you should (although you don't have to) say 'check' to warn him.

Demonstrate that White can get out of check by moving his king to a safe square, d2, e2 or f2. Now add a white rook on, say, d6. Demonstrate that White can also get out of check by interposing the rook on d1 so that his king is no longer under attack. Next, replace the white rook with a bishop on e5. This time White can get out of check by capturing the rook with his bishop.

Repeat that there are three ways to get out of check: move your king to a safe square, block the check (you can only do this if the check is from a queen, rook or bishop – why?) or capture the checking piece. Emphasise, with an example, that you can capture the checking piece with your king as long as it leaves your king on a safe square (some people think you cannot do this). You can use a mnemonic for the three ways to get out of check: ABC (Avoid or move Away, Block, Capture).

Many children instinctively reach for their king when they're in check, when it would often be better to capture or interpose rather than move the king.

Now set up a position with white king on e1, black king on e8 and black rooks on b2 and a1. Ask if White can get out of check. Once you've agreed that White cannot get out of check, explain that if you're in check and have no way out it's checkmate. Repeat that checkmate is a position in which one player is in check and cannot get out of check. The player who checkmates his opponent wins the game. The player who is checkmated loses the game. This is how you win a game of 'big chess'.

Set up a few more checkmate positions yourself, and ask your pupils to find some checkmate positions and demonstrate them to you. You might mention at this point that 'mate' and 'checkmate' mean the same thing, just like, for example, 'phone' and 'telephone'.

Now set up this position: white king on e1, black king on e3, black queen on d3. It's White's move. What can he play? Explain that White is not in check but cannot move any of his pieces. When this happens it is stalemate and the result of the game is a draw. (Make it clear that this is unlike our Capture the Flag rules in which you win if your opponent cannot move.)

These concepts need to be reinforced through examples and quizzes until the students are familiar with them.

Although there are one or two more rules to learn, you can if you wish start playing full games of chess. There will be more about how to do this in a later chapter.

9

OTHER RULES

If your children already know the rules you might want to start the course here, just to make sure you really do know some of the more complicated rules.

The most important rule we have to deal with at this point is castling.

Before you explain the rule make sure that you can do so accurately. Many social players have misapprehensions about the castling rule.

Emphasise that there are two reasons for castling: to make the king safe and to bring the rook into play. You should usually try to castle early on in your games. The king is usually safer on the king side, nearer the corner and away from the centre, which often gets opened up at the start of the game.

At this stage we also repeat the pawn promotion rule. Again there are many misconceptions about this: notably many social players erroneously believe you can only promote to a captured piece (so cannot have more than one queen).

We also teach (or repeat) the *en passant* rule. Many children find this very hard to understand. It may need regular repetition until it's understood. Children sometimes ask 'Are we playing the *en passant* rule?' Of course – it's part of chess so it should be 'played' in every game.

Finally we look at other ways to draw. We already know about stalemate. It's also an automatic draw if a position is reached where neither player can possibly deliver checkmate. Typically, this will be king against king, king against knight or king against bishop. This is often referred to as a draw by insufficient (mating) material. Many people mistakenly think that 'stalemate' is another word for draw. Children will often reach king against king and announce 'stalemate'.

You can also draw by agreement at any time. There's no need to mention this until children start playing in tournaments, though: it's better that they play out every game to the end: checkmate, stalemate or draw by insufficient material.

There are also two types of draw which are frequently misunderstood and mistaught. Children don't really need to know these until they start playing in tournaments, but they may well meet children in chess clubs who (think they) know them.

'Draw by repetition' can be claimed if the same position occurs three times with the same player to move. When they're losing, children sometimes arrange to play the same move three times and then claim a draw. No – certainly not! Note that it's repetition of position, not repetition of moves. The position may well be repeated three times because both players make the same moves but this is not necessarily the case.

The 50 move rule is often also misunderstood. This rule states that you can claim a draw if 50 moves have been played by both players without a pawn move or a capture being made. Note firstly that, although it's usually invoked where one player only has a king left, it can happen at any time in the game. Note secondly that whenever a pawn is moved or a capture is made you start counting again. Note thirdly that it's 50 moves each, not 25 moves each. Many children think (or have been taught) that when your opponent only has a king left you have to mate him in 25 moves.

10

YOUR FIRST GAMES

This is the most important chapter of all. If your children get off to a good start when they play their first games they will make rapid progress. If they start the wrong way and develop bad habits, both in thinking and in playing, it will be very hard to break them later.

You don't need to be able to play well yourself to help your children, but you do need to be able to recognise good play when you see it, and to differentiate good play from bad play.

We start by considering the respective strengths of the pieces. A very popular 'point count' which is much used by children and novices values the pawn as worth 1 point, the knight and bishop 3 points each, the rook as 5 points and the queen as 9 points. This is only a very rough guide and real values can go up and down like shares on the Stock Exchange depending on other factors, but it's still useful at this level. In fact it undervalues the queen by some way, and, to a lesser extent, the bishop. Many children enjoy counting up the points they and their opponent have won to see who's ahead. This can be encouraged (it also helps their maths!) but as the game goes on it's often easier to count what's left on the board rather than what's been taken. Children will often say 'I'm winning by two points'. It's better to get them to think more precisely about the material situation and say 'I'm ahead by a knight for a pawn'.

So we teach these values and, at the same time, make it clear that (other things, as usual, being equal) we should avoid losing points. Novices will often refuse, for example, to trade a knight for an enemy rook, because 'I don't want to lose my knight', even though they'll happily tell you that a knight is worth 3 points and a rook 5 points. If this is a problem, ask if they would swap £3 for £5, or three chocolates for five chocolates. Even players with several years' experience playing in tournaments will sometimes deliberately give up, for instance, a bishop for a pawn, saying 'It doesn't matter: I often win when I'm a bishop down'. You might like to reinforce this by introducing forfeits for anyone (parents as well as children) who plays a move losing material/points!

It must be emphasised that, in its simplest terms, the underlying logic of chess is that (other things being equal) Superior Force Wins. Many children play for years without understanding this, which is why they make little progress and the rest of the game makes little sense to them. There's no point in showing tactics to win pieces if they don't realise that winning pieces will help them win the game.

We then move onto the three vital concepts of Attack, Defence and Safety. For children who have come through the complete course, these ideas will already be familiar, but we now look at them within the context of the whole game.

Fig. 63

Demonstrate the position shown in Fig. 63. Ask how many black pawns the white queen is attacking? Then ask, for each pawn in turn, whether or not it's defended. They should see that the queen is attacking three pawns: h7 (defended by the rook on h8), f7 (defended by the king) and e5 (not defended). Explain the difference between an attack and a threat: an attack is something you *could* do while a threat is something you *want* to do. Therefore, according to the principle of SFW, Black should defend the e-pawn. Explain the concept of Attacker – Target – Defender.

Fig. 64

Now demonstrate Fig. 64. Ask what White is threatening. Although the knight is defended (twice) it's still threatened because it's more valuable than the pawn. If Black doesn't move the knight he'll lose 3 points and only gain one in return. So he must move the knight. If a stronger piece threatens a weaker piece it can be defended. But if a weaker piece threatens a stronger piece, unless the attack can be blocked or the attacking piece captured, the stronger piece must move away.

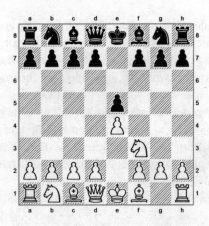

Fig. 65

Our third principle after Attack and Defence is Safety. What do you do before you cross the road? You look both ways to check that it's safe. If you don't do this you might get knocked down by a car. It's the same thing when you play chess. You have to look in all directions and make sure your move is safe before playing it. This is much harder because you have to see something that is not at the moment in front of your eyes. In Fig. 65, it wouldn't be safe for Black to move his queen to g5 or h4 because of the white knight on f3. You might want to demonstrate other ways of playing 'unsafe' moves, for instance moving a defender, moving a pinned piece, closing a line of defence, but, with younger children, it's probably best to leave this until later.

We also need to look at the concept of exchanging like for like: a trade of two identical pieces or of a bishop for a knight. We can consider our advantage or disadvantage in terms of points but we can also think about it in terms of ratio. There's not much difference between an army of 999 men and an army of 1,000 men, but if 998 men on each side get killed, you're left with an army of one man against an army of two men, which is twice the size.

So, in principle, if we're ahead on points we're trying to trade pieces and if we're behind we're trying to avoid trades. But if we're only a knight or a bishop up we often need to promote a pawn or two, so it's a good idea to make sure we don't run out of pawns.

(Beware of a possible ambiguity here: depending on context, 'pieces' may mean all your army or just the big guys as opposed to the pawns. You might need to provide clarification on occasion. If you say 'put your pieces away when you've finished the game' you obviously mean all of them, but if you say 'develop all your pieces in the opening' you only mean the big guys.)

So, if we're ahead we usually try to trade off the big guys, perhaps exchange a few pawns to give our remaining big guys space to move about, but, if necessary, keep some pawns on the board in case we need another queen or two.

Conversely, if we're behind we're trying to keep our remaining big guys while perhaps trading the enemy pawns.

11

SIMPLE CHECKMATES

This is the point where children should start checkmate training. Solving checkmate puzzles on a regular basis is very beneficial, not just so that you learn the basic mating patterns, but for developing chessboard vision and an understanding of how different pieces work together.

Most games at beginner level finish with one of two checkmate types.

The first type involves a mate with a rook or queen on the side of the board.

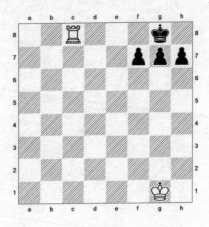

Fig. 66

In Fig. 66 the escape squares are all occupied by black pawns. This is a very common checkmate against the castled king.

Fig. 67

In the position in Fig. 67 two escape squares are occupied by black pawns, the third is controlled by the white bishop.

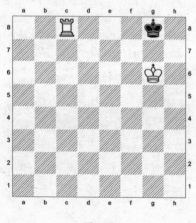

Fig. 68

In Fig. 68 the white king controls the escape squares: don't forget that two kings can never stand on adjacent squares.

The other checkmate involves a queen on the next square to the enemy king, supported by a friendly piece (and, of course, safe from capture by any enemy piece).

Fig. 69

Note that in Fig. 69 the white queen is one square vertically away from the black king and is supported by the white king. (Of course, if the king is on the side of the board the queen will need to be one square away horizontally.)

Fig. 70

With the enemy king in the corner in Fig. 70 the queen can also be diagonally adjacent. Here, she's supported by a friendly pawn.

Fig. 71

The queen can also be diagonally adjacent if the escape square is blocked by an enemy piece (or controlled by a friendly piece). In the position in Fig. 71 the queen is supported by the bishop, and the black queen blocks the king's escape.

Invite your children to set up their own checkmate positions using these ideas and set up positions yourself where they have to find the mating move.

At this point it's also worthwhile for children to learn the two rooks checkmate. Starting from the position in Fig. 72, we force checkmate by using the rooks in turn to force the black king to the edge of the board. If the black king approaches one of our rooks we need to be careful: we can either move the endangered rook to the other side of the board or use the rooks to defend each other. Children often find it difficult to find one or other of these plans.

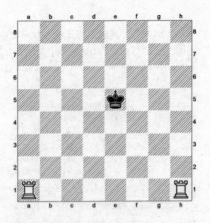

Fig. 72

Children should be encouraged to spend five minutes or so every day solving Mate in 1 and other one-move puzzles. Sources for these puzzles and advice on how to solve them are covered in Chapter 13 of Part One, and the Resources chapter.

12

OPENING STRATEGY

At this level, strategy involves finding good squares for your pieces. It's very important that you find good squares for your pieces at the start of the game: opening strategy.

Many children's chess development is held back because their parents display poor opening strategy against them, and they repeat the same mistakes in their games.

We'll look at each piece in turn.

For obvious reasons we need to keep the king safe from attack. Many beginners keep their king in the centre and attack from the sides. This is not to be recommended. We're usually going to castle early, probably on the king side where the king is nearer the corner and so safer from attack. If there has been, or might be, a pawn exchange in the centre this is especially important. We're going to keep a wall of pawns in front of the king and other pieces round about to defend him. If you like, think of the king as being like the goal in football.

The queen is our strongest attacking piece so we need to be careful how we use her. We know that little guys can chase big guys around so, generally speaking, we're not going to bring the queen out too soon because she'll be bossed around by enemy pawns, knights and bishops. But on the other hand, because of her power we can sometimes use her early in the game to win material, perhaps by means of a fork. Quite often we'll just nudge her up one square to 'connect the rooks'. Once a few minor pieces (bishops and knights) have been traded off we can often, as long as we're careful, make a lot more use of Her Majesty.

Many beginners feel sorry for their rooks stuck in the corner and try to bring them out early on by moving their a- and h-pawns two squares at the start of the game. This is a seriously bad idea. Rooks are clumsy early on and, even more than the queen, will get bossed around by bishops, knights and pawns. What rooks like best are open files (files with no pawns) and half-open files (files where we don't have a pawn). If you've played the Capture the Flag rook games you'll know that rooks can cause havoc by controlling an open file, moving into enemy territory, usually the seventh rank, and capturing a lot of pawns. So we try to connect the rooks early on by castling and developing (moving out) our other pieces. Then we move them to (potential) open or half-open files. You'll sometimes need to keep one rook back to prevent a snap mate on the back rank.

The best pieces to bring out early on are bishops and knights – strong enough to do damage but not so strong that they'll be chased round the board. Usually, we'll move our central pawns and then bring the bishops out along the open diagonals. Some players like to develop bishops on g2/g7 and/or b2/b7, (developing a bishop like this is called a fianchetto) but this requires more sophisticated play and is less suitable for beginners.

The knights, like the bishops, want to come out near the start of the game. The king's knights will usually go to f3 and f6, the queen's knights often to c3/c6 but sometimes, if we want to use the c-pawn to fight for the centre, to d2/d7. Knights like nothing more than squares in enemy territory near the centre of the board where they are safe from eviction by opposing pawns.

We're going to use our centre pawns: our d- and e-pawns, and sometimes also our c-pawn to fight for and control the centre. Just as in football, control of the midfield will often lead to an advantage because pieces in that area of the board can readily reach anywhere they want to go. If we castle on the king-side our f-, g- and h-pawns are going to stay at home to provide a defensive shield for our king. Our a- and b-pawns will probably stay at home early on, but may later be used to gain space and attack on the queen-side. Many beginners make random moves with their king-side pawns at the start of the game. Children enjoy learning Fool's Mate, a graphic example of what can happen if you do this: 1. f2-f3 e7-e5 2. g2-g4 Qd8-h4 which is a drastic – and the quickest possible – checkmate. We also have a choice to make with our pawns: should we avoid exchanges, which makes the opening easy to play but the middle-game harder, or should we try to trade pawns and open up the position for our pieces, when it will be easier to think of what to do but also easier to make oversights when pieces are flying round the board?

You can try to explain this by playing through a few moves with your children. With younger children, just show them the moves and see if they can remember them. Older children will be able to deal with the explanations as well.

White starts by moving from e2 to e4. He's occupying the centre and opening lines for his bishop and queen. Black does the same thing: moving from e7 to e5. (Other moves are possible for both sides but these moves are most suitable for beginners.) Now White's usual move is to develop his king's knight: Ng1-f3. (Fig. 73.)

Fig. 73

White has a threat which, according to SFW, we must meet. In fact it's also good – as long as you know what you're doing – to create a threat ourselves by playing Ng8-f6, but such counter-attacks can often backfire. Let's say we decide to defend the threatened pawn. We don't like Bf8-d6 (blocks the d-pawn and places the bishop on an ineffectual square). We also don't care much for Qd8-e7 or Qd8-f6, both bringing the queen out too soon, with the former move blocking the bishop and the latter move confining the knight on g8. We should also rule out f7-f6, again taking away the best square from the knight as well as weakening the king's defences. It's OK to play d7-d6, even though it blocks in the bishop slightly, but the usual move is Nb8-c6. (Fig. 74.)

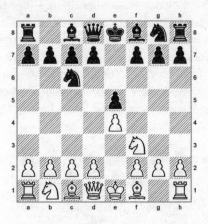

Fig. 74

No threat, so White has a free choice. All we'll say here is that there are four sensible moves. Nb1-c3 is simple and good. There are two strong bishop moves: Bf1-c4 places the bishop on an active square attacking the pawn on f7, and Bf1-b5 attacks the knight on c6 which is in turn defending the pawn on e5. Finally, White, having worked out that it's safe to do so, can open up the position in the centre by playing d2-d4. For younger children, it's best to leave it here for now. If you want to follow this exercise any further with older children you could use the opening moves we looked at in the previous chapter.

13
SIMPLE TACTICS

At this point we can reinforce again the principle that Superior Force Wins, and the principles of Attack, Defence and Safety.

So what happens is that we make a threat and our opponent meets it: he makes a threat and we meet it. If we want to win material we have to be more subtle than this.

We look first at the idea of two pieces attacking the same enemy target. This is sometimes, confusingly, referred to as a double attack. It's better to think of it as a team attack or a gang attack.

We can often use this technique to attack enemy pawns. It's easy to miss because you have to see how the pieces are working together.

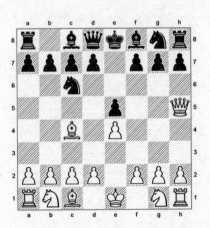

Fig. 75

In Fig. 75 White has just moved his bishop to c4. It's very easy for beginners just to look at the bishop, and to forget that the queen is also attacking f7. The f-pawn is attacked twice but only defended once so Black has to meet the threat. He can do this safely by moving his queen to e7 or f6 to provide an extra defender for his pawn, or by moving his pawn to g6 to block off the queen. If he misses the threat, White will deliver checkmate by taking on f7 with his queen. You saw this checkmate in the previous chapter. This checkmate (Scholar's Mate) is very popular at primary school level: make sure this is understood and that your pupils know how to prevent it.

We now move onto double threats. Children who have played the mini-games will be familiar with some of these concepts already. Explain that if you make a threat your opponent will probably be able to defend, but if you play a move that makes two threats at the same time your opponent may only be able to meet one of the threats. You might demonstrate how you can win a game of Noughts and Crosses in the same way.

Ask them to explain the idea of a fork: a double threat (NOT a double attack) with one piece in two directions. All pieces can do forks, but queen and knight forks happen most often because they can move in eight directions.

Fig. 76

Fig. 76 is an example of a queen fork at the start of the game. Black has just moved his queen to a5, checking the white king and threatening the bishop on g5. Demonstrate that White cannot save the bishop because the pawn on e3 has closed the c1-h6 diagonal.

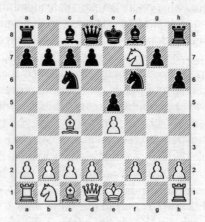

Fig. 77

Knight forks often happen early in the game on f2/f7 (forking queen and rook, as in Fig. 77) and on c2/c7 (forking king and rook).

Fig. 78

Pins are quite hard to explain to children. In Fig. 78 all four knights are pinned at the moment. The knights on c3 and c6 are pinned to the king and therefore not allowed to move. The knights on f3 and f6 are pinned to the queen. They are allowed to move, but if they do so they'll leave their queen to be captured. It's important to recognise this scenario. Many games are lost by moving a pinned knight in this sort of position, often because children automatically pick up the knight because they're scared of having it taken by the bishop.

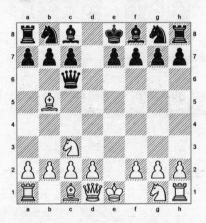

Fig. 79

There are other pins that win material. This will typically be a rook pinning a queen against a king, or a bishop pinning a rook or a queen (as in Fig. 79) against a king.

Our last tactical idea is the discovered attack/discovered check. This involves moving a piece to open a line of attack, while the piece that is moved creates another threat.

In Fig. 80, if White moves his knight from e5 his queen will check the black king. When a piece moves out of the way so that another piece checks the enemy king it's known as a discovered check. If he moves the knight to c6 he'll create a second threat:

Fig. 80

to take the black queen. Black will have to get out of check and cannot do so without losing his queen.

PART THREE
YOUR NEXT MOVE

1

JOINING A CLUB

If your children have understood and can put into practice everything in this course they'll be able to play a reasonable game of chess. They'll know the rules of the game, be able to put their pieces on reasonably effective squares, and, most importantly, understand the principle that Superior Force (usually) Wins and be able to make a good stab at playing a simple game without making one-move blunders.

In fact, this is what I would consider to be the minimum entry requirement for a 'playing' chess club rather than a tuition group for beginners/novices. At this level you'll be able to enjoy playing good games with your friends and have some sort of low level understanding of what's happening rather than just playing random moves.

If your children's school runs a chess club this is probably where you'll start. Primary school chess clubs usually meet for an hour after school, but some schools prefer lunchtime clubs and a few run clubs before school. Some schools employ professional chess teachers while others use teachers or parents to run their clubs. If your school doesn't have a chess club perhaps you could encourage them to start one. Alternatively, your children could take a chess set into school and find some friends who would like a game.

Children who have fully grasped everything in the course will probably, with a bit of practice, do well as most children in most school chess clubs have been taught the moves at home by parents who know little about the game themselves and have not (yet) read this book!

It may well be that this is as far as your children want to go: they enjoy playing the occasional game, maybe once a week, but don't want to take the game any further than that. If so, that's absolutely fine and I would expect that most children would want to stop here. Ask them the question, though. Give them the choice. Otherwise you'll never know.

Some children, however, will say 'Hey, chess is a really great game. I'd like to try to play for my school, my club, my county, my country. I'd like to become a Grandmaster, or maybe even world champion.' If this is their dream, you owe it to your children to try to make it come true. If your children are winning most of their games against their contemporaries at school, you should certainly encourage them to take this route.

If your children are ambitious they'll probably need to join an outside chess club. There are many chess clubs for adults which meet in the evenings but these are, for various reasons, unsuitable for most young children. Instead, you should look for a junior chess club. Some areas are well provided with junior chess clubs but in other parts of the country you may have to travel quite a long way. These clubs will meet either early evening or at weekends, will typically be of longer duration than school chess clubs (an hour and a half, or sometimes longer), and, while some are run by volunteers, others will be run by professional chess teachers. Joining a junior chess club will give your children the opportunity to meet other children who share their interest in chess and make new friends. They should be more serious than school chess clubs: you should expect the club to be well organised, the children to be quiet and well-behaved, and serious tuition and competitions should be provided for those children who are strong enough to benefit. Children will be encouraged to learn to use clocks and record their games on scoresheets.

They'll still need to practise regularly at home. Now they can play a reasonable game, if they don't have anyone to play at home they could consider playing on the internet. There are many sites where you can play either turn-based or real-time games, although young children using the internet will, of course, require an appropriate level of adult supervision and instruction about online safety.

You'll remember the three stages of children's chess development: Vision, Calculation, Judgement. Children will still need to solve puzzles regularly, but will be moving onto the puzzles designed to develop and test calculation skills. This means Mate in 2 (or more) puzzles along with simple two-move tactics.

Children will also need to know some basic endings: how to force checkmate with king and queen against king, and with king and rook against king, as well as some simple king and pawn endings.

The openings have been studied for as long as chess has been played and an extensive body of knowledge has been built up over the centuries. With the explosion of literature on chess openings and the rapid dissemination of information via the internet this has expanded dramatically over the past few decades. Any serious player has no choice but to tap into this knowledge. There's no way you're going to work it all out for yourself, and a player who has not studied the openings will stand little or no chance against someone who has.

If you're just playing at primary school level you don't need to know very much: just some basic knowledge of the openings starting 1. e4 e5 (the most suitable openings for less experienced players) will suffice. If you decide you want to take the game further, though, there will be a lot more work to do. Many children spend far too much time learning openings (and many teachers spend far too much time teaching openings) before they need to do so. At this point, spending time on developing tactical skills and learning endings is more important. Parents often ask me to teach their children some openings, or, even worse, show them some traps, before a forthcoming tournament. Such short-termism is not to be encouraged, though. Your children may win a game or two in their next tournament, but it will be at the cost of long-term development, as, when your children get stronger and meet stronger opponents, the traps will no longer work.

All this information and more is readily available in many formats, for instance via the Intermediate Lessons tab on chessKIDS academy (www.chesskids.org.uk or www.chesskids.me.uk).

Serious tournaments involve the use of chess clocks. Children should have the opportunity to get used to using both digital and analogue clocks with games played at different (fast and slow) time limits before taking part in tournaments. When presented with a clock for the first time children will usually panic and play much too fast. Typically, you'll have 30 minutes on your clock to play all your moves in a game. This will give you about 45 to 60 seconds per move which is more than enough for players at this level, but you need to get used to this before facing it in a tournament. As children develop their calculation and judgement skills, learn to look further ahead, consider more alternatives, and assess positions more deeply they'll need more time than that, but, for most children, that will be a few years away, assuming they want to take that route.

It's also a good idea at this stage if children get used to using scoresheets to record their own games. This is not usually required in lower level junior tournaments or 'rapidplay' tournaments with 30 minutes or so on the clock for each player, but is compulsory in higher level competitions with slower time limits. If you're not used to it you'll probably spend all your time concentrating on your notation rather than thinking about the position. With a bit of practice it will become second nature, but that practice should take place at a chess club or at home before you have to do it in tournaments.

If you're really ambitious you'll want to use your scoresheets to analyse your game with a stronger player. It's children who are eager to reach the top who will benefit most from a private chess tutor, and one of the things he or she will (or should) want to do is analyse your games with you.

2

PLAYING IN A TOURNAMENT

If your children are at all serious about chess, at some point they'll want to have a go at playing in a tournament. Many schools in the UK run heats of the UK Chess Challenge during the spring term. The top boy and top girl in each age group qualify for their county Megafinal, which is for many children their introduction to tournament chess, and where they'll compete against children who have qualified from other schools in their county. Children who do well in this event (and if your children have understood everything in this book they'll stand a chance) will then progress to the North of England or South of England Gigafinal, and from then potentially to the Terafinal, where the top children in each age group compete against each other for a substantial cash prize. Alternatively, there might be an open junior tournament in your area. Those living in or near London might take part in a qualifying tournament for the London Junior Championships during the autumn term.

There's no particular advantage in entering children into tournaments of this nature before they're ready (remember the story of the boy who thought knights couldn't jump) and you can't necessarily expect your children to do well in their first event, but if they know and can put into practice everything in this book they'll be able to give a good account of themselves.

Even so, playing in a tournament for the first time can be quite daunting so it's as well to know what to expect.

Your children might be feeling either anxious or excited before the tournament, but you should still make sure that they get a good night's sleep and get up in time for a light breakfast before setting out in plenty of time. There's nothing worse than arriving late for a competition, leaving your children flustered and in a state of panic before they even start their game, and if they're playing with clocks they will be penalised. Clocks are started on time: if you're late, tough. So make sure you know exactly where you're going and how to get there before you set out. Make allowances for traffic jams or train cancellations: it's better to be too early than too late.

On arrival check the layout of the venue. Find out where the toilets are. The boards will be numbered: check that you understand the numbering system so that you can find your board number easily. Parents may or may not be allowed to watch their children playing. Even if you are allowed, it's best not to do so. Your children will be under a lot of pressure anyway and having someone hovering over the board watching their every move isn't going to help. There will be an analysis room or area where parents will be able to wait. There will probably be some chess sets there as well for friendly games or analysis between rounds. There will be a table at the front of the playing room where you'll find the tournament organisers and arbiters (the chess equivalent of referees or umpires).

Your children should, obviously, be aware of the rules of chess, including the *en passant* rule. If they're not sure, go through it every day until they know and understand it.

Make sure your children understand the 'touch and move' rule. They should have had experience of this at school or at their chess club but it is still often misunderstood. If you touch a piece deliberately, with the intention of moving it, you have to move it. If you touch an opponent's piece deliberately, with the intention of taking it, either with your hand or with your piece, you have to take it. If it's not possible to move or take the piece you touched there is no penalty. If you wish to adjust a piece which isn't in the centre of the square you may do so by saying 'Adjust' or '*J'adoube*' (French for 'I dub') BEFORE you touch it. Many children think – or hope – you can pick up a piece, decide you don't want to move it, say 'adjust' and move something else instead. Certainly not! I've also seen children say that their move was a joke and try to take it back. If someone tries one of these tricks against your children, they shouldn't let them get away with it. If they have a problem of any sort, or if anything happens they don't understand, they should raise their hand and call an arbiter. Using 'Adjust' at all can often lead to misunderstandings because your opponent doesn't hear you so the best advice is never to use it at all. Your children should make sure all the pieces are in the centre of their squares at the start of the game and, when they make a move, ensure that they place the piece carefully in the centre of the square.

If playing in a higher level tournament it will also pay to be familiar with the 'two minute' rule. This applies only in certain tournaments, depending on the time control. The rule states that, if you have two minutes or less on the clock and your opponent is not trying to win the game by normal means you can claim a draw. The way you do this is by offering a draw, and, if your opponent refuses, calling an arbiter and making the claim to him/her. Your claim will usually only be accepted if you are lots of material ahead or in a totally drawn ending. Even if you have a winning position, if there's a chance that you might make a mistake your claim won't be upheld. You certainly can't do it whenever you're down to the last two minutes. The arbiter can (and should) give your opponent extra time if you make a frivolous claim.

There are various other forms of sharp practice that children often try on in junior tournaments. You can, if you like, offer a draw if you think the position's level. If you're using clocks the only correct time to offer a draw is in between making your move and pressing your clock. Offering a draw at any other time might be considered to be distracting your opponent. Many young players continue offering a draw every two or three moves after it's been declined. This again is distracting. If an opponent does this against your child, he would be entirely justified in raising his hand to call an arbiter to complain. If a draw offer has been turned down it should not be offered again unless the position has radically changed. The opponent knows the situation and will offer a draw himself if he changes his mind in a few moves' time. Note that a draw is ONLY offered because you think the position's equal. Offering a draw because you're losing and hope your opponent will accept is both bad manners and distracting. I've seen children offer a draw in a lost position and extend their hand. Their opponent, being well brought up, shakes hands and, before they realise what's happened the first player has filled in the result slip and handed it in as a draw, and there's nothing they can do about it. Again and again, if your child is not sure what's going on, he should raise his hand and an arbiter will come and help him. The best advice on draw offers for less experienced players is not to offer them at all, and to think twice before accepting a draw offer. It may be better to play the game out: even if you lose you'll learn something from it.

In most tournaments there's a result slip to fill out and hand in at the end of the game, giving the names of the players, the round and board numbers, and the result. It's important this is done correctly. It's very easy to put the 'white' and 'black' names the wrong way round. It's also very easy to forget to fill in the result. The players should write their full name, not just their first name, so that the controllers will easily be able to identify the players. The result slip is another source of sharp practice. It's the winner's responsibility to hand it in, but I've seen children who have lost the game take the slip on the pretence of being helpful and change the result before submitting it.

The pairings for the first round will be displayed five or ten minutes before the start time. If the pairings are done by hand they'll be displayed on cards slotted into a large board, or if they're done by computer it's more likely to be a notice stuck to the wall. The players with White will be on your left and the players with Black on your right, with the board number in the middle. There will also be a number on each player's card: this is the tournament number, NOT the board number! You don't need to know this: it's purely for the convenience of the organisers. Oh, and whatever you do, don't interrupt the organisers to ask the time of the next round or when the pairings will be ready while they're in the middle of working them out. Believe me, it's really annoying!

Most tournaments are run on the Swiss System. All players play all rounds – you don't get knocked out if you lose. There are three principles: (1) you cannot play the same player more than once in a tournament, (2) as far as possible you play someone on the same score as yourself and (3) as far as possible you equalise and alternate colours. If there are more white winners than black winners in your tournament, some winners will get a second white and some losers will get a second black. (Parents often complain when their children get a second black in a row, but never when they get a second white!) In more serious tournaments where most players have grades or ratings there's a fourth principle: within each score group the stronger half will play the weaker half. In most tournaments you score 1 point for a win, half a point for a draw and no points for a loss. In the heats of the UK Chess Challenge you score 3 points for a win, 2 for a draw and 1 for a loss. The Megafinals and higher levels prefer to use football scoring: 3 points for a win, 1 for a draw and nothing for a loss. The idea of the Swiss System is that players will eventually find their level and meet evenly matched opponents.

RESOURCES

This is inevitably a selective list. If you find something else you like, that's absolutely fine. There are many excellent resources not listed on here, but also much that's misleading or just incorrect.

Most of what you will require is only available from specialist chess dealers. The biggest UK chess dealer is the London Chess Centre (www.chess.co.uk) with an online shop as well as a retail outlet in central London. Many of the books recommended for beginners are excellent in themselves, but only suited to players with 20:20 chessboard vision and a sound appreciation of the game's logic, which, for most young children, takes two or three years to reach. Parents sometimes tell me their children have been put off chess by books which were too hard for them.

I'm rather sceptical about the value of starting very young children on chess, especially if the parents themselves are not chess players, but if you really want to do this you'll need *Chess is Child's Play* by Laura Sherman and Bill Kilpatrick (Mongoose Press), which follows an age-appropriate step by step course designed for children from age 2 upwards.

The most comprehensive chess course for children currently available in English is the Dutch Steps Method (www.stappenmethode.nl/en or www.chess-steps.com). This course has been used for many years in the Netherlands and is much used in many other West European countries. This is a six-year course based almost entirely on the development of tactical skills.

It comprises a series of workbooks for children along with manuals for teachers. Most of it has been translated into English, but the translation is not always good. Other volumes are available in either Dutch or German. The first three steps of the course are also available as interactive software under the name Chess Tutor.

The course is designed for use in small coaching groups comprising children of similar age and experience, which is very much not the way we do things over here. Even so, the worksheets are great for casual use. It would also be possible for parents and children to follow much of the course at home, but as the answers to the worksheets are in the teachers' manuals you'll need both.

Note that, at the time of writing, the Steps material is not available via Amazon, but can be purchased online at the addresses above or at the London Chess Centre.

If you're following a 'slow' sequential course, the other supply of pre-checkmate puzzles is the *Chess Camp* books by Igor Sukhin (Mongoose Press). At the time of writing there are seven volumes available, the first of which comprises one-move pre-checkmate puzzles while volumes 2 and 3 are both Mate in 1 puzzles. The puzzles in these books are also available as an app for iPad or iPhone.

Sukhin has for many years been a best-selling Russian author of elementary chess books for children. If you're using these books you'll probably also want *Gary's Adventures in Chess Country*, a great book for young beginners by the same author and publisher. Like my book *Chess for Kids* it uses a story to teach chess.

Another Russian 'slow' course is *Chess Gymnasium* by Grandmaster Jaan Ehlvest, based on the system that has been used in that part of the world for many years. It's available at www.chessgymnasium.com. This comprises a children's workbook and a teachers' manual, and is designed for use either at school or at home.

I also recommend the three volumes of *Chess Step by Step From Beginner to Champion* by Aleksandr Kitsis (Vivacity, Inc.), another course with a lot of very useful pre-checkmate, one-move and two-move puzzles for beginners and novices.

My website chessKIDS academy (www.chesskids.org.uk or www.chesskids.me.uk) includes a complete free multi-media chess course for children. This book, along with my book *Chess for Kids*, is designed to be used alongside the website. The hard copy version of the first stage of the course, incorporating worksheets, is available for free download under the title *Journey Through Chess*. Further worksheets and other coaching materials for beginners and novices are currently being developed: visit regularly for further information.

There are many well produced books for young children which take a faster route. If you find something you think your children will enjoy reading then go for it. One popular and excellent example is *Chess for Children* by Murray Chandler and Helen Milligan (Gambit Books). My previous book for children, *Move One!* (Faber & Faber) is long out of print but second hand copies are available.

Another excellent Russian source of one-move puzzles is *The Manual of Chess Combinations: Chess School 1A* by Sergei Ivashchenko, another best-selling chess author. Unlike Sukhin, he doesn't provide pre-checkmate puzzles. Unfortunately, at the time of writing it's not easy to get hold of any of the books from this series at a sensible price, although you may be able to find a download site. However, these books, and much more, including 77,000 Mate in 1 puzzles, are available on CD or for download at http://www.chessok.com – a highly recommended resource for novices who are old enough to use software of this nature.

If you're looking for chess software to teach chess to young children I recommend the Fritz and Chesster series published by ChessBase (http://www.chessbase-shop.com/en/categories /130).

There are many DVDs available for beginners but do ensure that they don't go too fast for young children. I'd particularly recommend *Chess for Novices Volumes 1 and 2* by Sabrina Chevannes, again published by ChessBase.

There's a wide choice of puzzle books for children who have got past the 'Vision' stage of chess and are now in the 'Calculation' stage.

For children just into this stage, *Power Chess for Kids* by Charles Hertan (New in Chess) will get you off to a good start in learning how to calculate two moves ahead.

My favourite puzzle books for children are the remarkable series by the Canadian chess teacher Jeff Coakley (Chess 'n' Math Association). *Winning Chess Strategy for Kids* shows you how to do it. *Winning Chess Exercises for Kids* offers 100 pages of puzzles of increasing difficulty. *Winning Chess Puzzles for Kids* (two volumes) give you a wide range of diverse puzzles, some easy, some very hard, designed to get you thinking about chess in different ways.

The celebrated American chess teacher Bruce Pandolfini has written many excellent books for children and novices on all aspects of the game.

For children who are ambitious to do well in tournaments, I recommend two books by Murray Chandler (Gambit Books). *How to Beat Your Dad at Chess* will teach you basic checkmate patterns and *Chess Tactics for Kids* will show you basic tactical ideas.

If you want to learn to play better chess yourself or you're looking for a chess book for older learners you could start with *How to Beat Your Kids at Chess* by David MacEnulty (Russell Enterprises Inc.): my top recommendation for adult beginners. An alternative which takes a faster pace is *The Right Way to Play Chess* by David Pritchard (Right Way Books). You might also like *Chess for Dummies* by James Eade (John Wiley & Sons) or *The Complete Idiot's Guide to Chess* by Patrick Wolff (Alpha Books).

An excellent general book on chess is *The Mammoth Book of Chess* by Graham Burgess (Mammoth Books). Although it's rather out of date now, you might also like to get hold of a second-hand copy of *The Even More Complete Chess Addict* by Mike Fox and Richard James (Faber & Faber) for chess history, trivia, anecdotes and humour.

For teachers or home educators the books by Alexey Root provide a lot of suggestions for cross-curricular links. Titles currently available are *Children and Chess*; *Science, Math, Checkmate*; *Read, Write, Checkmate*; *People, Places, Checkmate*; *The Living Chess Game* (all Greenwood Publishing Group); *Thinking with Chess* (Mongoose Press).

American teacher and writer Dan Heisman is one of the few who has a genuine understanding of the needs of the novice player. *A Guide to Chess Improvement* (Everyman Chess) is my main recommendation for adults who want to move beyond the basics. Two other books you will find useful are *Everyone's 2nd Chess Book* (Thinkers' Press) and *A Parent's Guide to Chess* (Russell Enterprises), even though the latter title is geared towards the US market.

A website you'll find very useful is www.chesskid.com which includes a large database of puzzles to be solved online, a chess computer which can be played at different levels, and the option of playing chess against other kids either in real time or turn-based (for example 3 days per move), although you have to pay to use most of the facilities.

A good free site where you can solve puzzles interactively is www.ideachess.com which has options for easy puzzles, many of which involve vision rather than calculation, and mates in one move. An excellent source of software and chess puzzles for novices is www.chessok.com.

If your children want to play online for free in a child-friendly environment you could try Yahoo Kids (http://kids.yahoo.com/games/game/chess). There are many other sites where you can play either in real time or via email (www.chess.com is a good place for either), but your children need to get beyond the beginner stage before they can really benefit from them.

If your children are interested in playing competitively your whole family should certainly watch the film *Innocent Moves* (the original US title was *Searching for Bobby Fischer*), based on the true story of American chess prodigy Josh Waitzkin and his journalist father Fred. You should also read the book on which the movie was based (*Searching for Bobby Fischer* by Fred Waitzkin (Penguin Books)).

Teachers interested in chess should also watch the documentary, *Brooklyn Castle* (2012), which tells the story of the remarkable chess achievements of a Brooklyn school (I.S.318). At the time of writing you can watch it online at http://www.movies77.net/watch-brooklyn-castle-online.html. Paul Tough's book, *How Children Succeed* (Houghton Mifflin Harcourt), also has a lot of information about this school. *Knights of the South Bronx* (2005) is a drama based on a similar story of chess at an inner-city New York school, although their achievements were somewhat exaggerated. It's currently only available for purchase with Region 1 encoding but it can be downloaded or watched online.

Finally, and most importantly, some online resources for parents and teachers in the UK.

If you're interested in promoting chess in your school, especially a primary school in a deprived area, you should certainly contact the wonderful charity Chess in Schools and Communities (visit their website at www.chessinschools.co.uk). Amongst other things, they run regular workshops up and down the country which will show you how best to run a school chess club.

Most schools who run chess clubs take part in the UK Chess Challenge (www.ukchesschallenge.com), described above. My one caveat is that many schools encourage children to enter this event before they're ready for competitive chess: the upside of this is that if your children have been taught well they'll get good results.

The English Chess Federation (www.englishchess.org.uk) runs national schools championships and also provides lists of chess coaches and junior chess clubs and organisers.

If you have any questions about this book, or specific enquiries about chess in the Richmond/Twickenham area, please feel free to email the author via the Contact page at www.chesskids.org.uk.

INDEX